AWAKENING THE SPIRITUAL HEART

Awakening the Spiritual Heart

How to Fall in Love with Life

ANDREAS ZIÖRJEN

Chakra-Atelier

Published by Chakra-Atelier
Bernstrasse 7, 3600 Thun, Switzerland
www.chakra-atelier.ch

ISBN Trade Paperback: 978-3-907242-22-3
ISBN E-Book: 978-3-907242-23-0

Cover Art, Artwork on Pages 34/155: Getty/NikkiZalewski. Created with Canva Pro.

First Printing, 2023

Contents

PART TWO
DEEPENING

ANNEX
RESOURCES

On the Chakra Series

W elcome, dear fellow explorer of reality, to this fourth volume in a series of meditation and philosophy books that aim to offer some new perspectives on the ancient spiritual truth telling us that we're not just brains in a body, but something more: energetic beings moving through a physical experience.

The chakra concept has been the backbone of my own practice for twenty-five years and has provided a reliable foundation for the transformational retreats I've been leading in various countries for the past ten years.

The tantric yoga practitioners of old weren't the only ones using similar concepts, although most people who have heard of energy centers today still know these structures by the name they gave them—chakras, a Sanskrit term meaning wheels or vortices.

The original tantrics, if we believe the ancient texts, simply noticed that there were blockages or knots in the central axis of most people's energy field—and that these knots somehow interfered with the free flow of energy that they associated with awakened consciousness.

The knots needed to be untangled so that *Kundalini Shakti*, our primal creative "soul force," could unwind, rise, and infuse the practitioner's entire being with Her power. I can't argue with this, as I felt it myself many years ago when I stepped into Oneness, and nothing has been the same in my life since, although I am still far from feeling like an awakened master.

The view of the chakras that I invite you to explore with me in this series is a bit unconventional. For one thing, we won't be moving through the structure in the usual linear way—from the bottom up, or sometimes from the top down. Rather, we'll be following a slightly different, but hopefully helpful, progression, hopping between the energy centers in a way that I feel will open your connection to and understanding of them in the easiest way possible.

In the early weekend seminars and week-long retreats on working with the chakras I taught, I first tried to move through the subtle energies of these centers as I had learned in my yoga and meditation teacher studies, starting by grounding in the root chakra and then moving upward.

I soon realized, however, that due to the fact that most of us are quite busy in our minds, it proved more helpful for many people to start with the more mentally accessible upper chakras and move downward to really achieve an experience of embodiment.

Later, we experimented with moving inward toward the heart from both sides, as well as starting with the heart as the soul center and moving outward. Nowadays, when I work with groups or individuals, we move through the centers in whatever way is needed to facilitate the easiest shift in consciousness, although starting in the heart center, in my experience, generally proves most effective for personal work.

The Chakra Series as a sequence of practice books for beginners and advanced students alike, begins by exploring willpower—in its first volume, *The Power of Sankalpa*, we focus on the solar plexus chakra. This makes sense because all practice—indeed, all human endeavor—begins with intention, and our intentions color everything that we may or may not experience in the areas governed by the other chakras. Furthermore, this is the place where we can strengthen and stabilize our ego —something we cannot do without to safely travel the path of the mystic later on, in the uppermost chakras.

Volume 2, called *Be YOU to the Max*, addresses the areas of life that are connected to the throat chakra. This chakra is number five in the classical *shat chakra* system and an intimate partner to the solar plexus. It is the place where the intentions formed by our will and ego are allowed to manifest—or not. The throat is the power center of permission. Harmonizing the energy in this area is a prerequisite for achieving more freedom in our lives.

In the third book in the series, *Walking the Path of the Mystics*, we work with the power of our awareness—*buddhi*, for yogis—in the two upper classical chakras. These are the Third Eye between the eyebrows and the crown chakra, which governs our connection to the Divine. We need the discernment of the third eye chakra and the trust in something "higher" than us that the crown chakra offers in order to descend further into embodiment. The blockages and patterns that are stored in the lower chakras, and, to a lesser extent, in the energetic armor that many of us carry around our hearts, are very dense, and we need a lot of clarity of mind and a well-trained ability to discriminate in order not to get lost in them if we really want to go deep.

In the volume you are holding, Book Four of the series, we will explore the energies of the spiritual and energetic heart—the center of our soul core, whose dominant qualities are spaciousness and, as a natural result, love and bliss.

Books Five and Six, finally, will center on the "lowest" and most physically oriented of the chakras, addressing the topic of bringing the ease, acceptance and clarity of the higher chakras into full, embodied expression.

The famous Swiss psychologist C.G. Jung is said to have remarked that he had hardly met anyone who was truly fully incarnated, that is, who had reached their full potential in the Root Chakra.

Therefore, in the final books of the series, which have only been partially written at this time, we will address trust—which is the predominant quality of the Root— and the whole subject of sexual creative energy in the Sacral.

If you should find this exposition a bit daunting in its complexity: Don't worry. I've given you the full context for yoga professionals here, but the books themselves are largely designed to be as easy to read as possible, as much of their content is based on my workshops and short ten-day audio course formats that introduce the chakras to beginners. Many of the core ideas of my specific "flavor" of chakra work are revisited regularly throughout the series and presented from different angles, allowing for easy integration.

Also, each book can be read independently of the others, as all relevant concepts are explained in the way that is most helpful for understanding the role of the book's focus chakra in the larger picture.

May you be blessed by the Light, and may the ideas contained in these practice manuals contribute to the ever-expanding field of love, bliss and clarity that is woven through this beautiful world of ours. May we all expand as well, into the full, blooming power of our True Nature.

Andreas Hau'oli Ziörjen

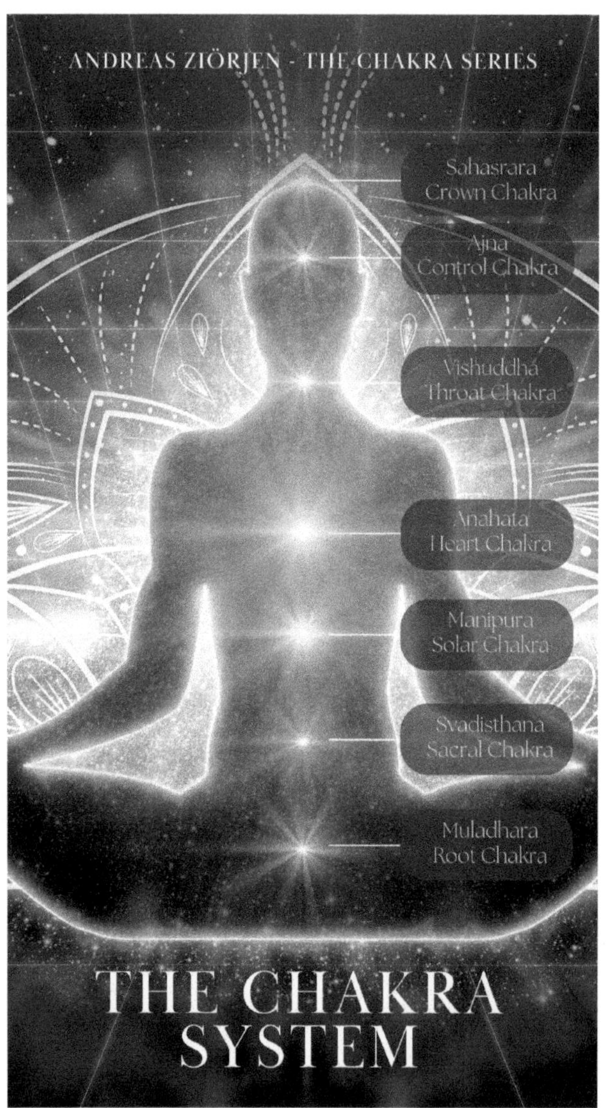

The Chakra System
Created with Canva Pro. Artwork: Getty/Activedia

Introduction

Can you remember what it feels like to be in love? And, can you remember how it feels when that love is then even finding resonance with the person(s) you're in love with?

For most of us, everything then becomes more connected, more colorful, more sensual and more joyful—life is simply that little bit more beautiful than usual.

This sensation of being in love with another person is pretty similar to how it feels when we connect deeply with our heart chakra.

And even better: the archetypal form of love for all being that you can access through working with your heart chakra holds a kind of clarity and unconditionality that falling in love with another human usually cannot offer. This is because, in interpersonal relationships, we are usually confronted with a multitude of subconscious beliefs and ideas that cloud our vision—no matter how good things seem at the moment and how much love hormones happen to flow through our bodies and brains.

Where do those beliefs and ideas that are clouding the pure love shining forth from our spiritual hearts come from? Consider the following, possible explanation: Beginning in our early childhood, we have been taught many concepts and inner images about love. Those concepts and images came to us through words, subtle energies, sounds, and, mostly, the actions and re-actions of the beings who were important to us when we were small, like parents, caregivers, or teachers.

Thus, we've been subconsciously programmed with an inner imprint of what love means for other people, and this imprint is still at work in our subconscious. Ideally, during puberty we've been able to add some of our own imprints that may be at least slightly closer to our own soul core. That is, if we were lucky.

But even in that period of our lives, we were still bombarded by concepts telling us how to love. "All you need is love", "Make love, not war", "Love your neighbor as yourself", and so on. It's obviously very difficult to develop our own take on the topic, if we're continuously receiving input all purporting one specific kind of subjective "truth".

Advertising, stories, movies, religion, the example of the people around us—all this has contributed to the fact that in most of us, an overall rather diffuse image of what love actually is has solidified and been stored as a sort of template in our subconscious.

There are things like love for one or more partners, for parents, friends, and, of course not least, self-love. Many people will probably agree that without self-love, we cannot really love others.

However, love is not—or at least not only—to be equated with things like acceptance, attraction, partnership, intimacy or benevolence.

There are less clearly positive but culturally/religiously often deeply rooted subconscious aspects to it as well, like unreflective devotion, sacrifice or self-sacrifice, coupling "love" with performance or conditions, or even the threat of spiritual/religious punishment if one does not "love" in the right way.

How do *you* feel about the concept of love? You may want to think about this for a moment.

As for myself, when I started to work with heart energies in my yoga practice about ten years ago, I had to realize that I didn't really know for myself in any depth what was behind this term—and that was in spite of the fact that I had already said the words "I love you" to quite a few people in my life, and also had lived some deep mystical experiences in which what I'd called "love" had been very present.

In the years since, exploring what love in both the spiritual and an embodied sense really means has become an important part of my practice. In this book, I will share the practical findings from this inner research with you.

Quite easy to grasp is the afore-mentioned feeling of being in love—something almost everyone who's ever been a teenager will know.

It's when our hormones are running wild, confusion reigns our brains and love can be equaled with the desire to be with the other person in the most intense way possible. However, we all know that being *in love* with someone or something does not necessarily have to be the same as *loving* them—even though it can be.

As for me, about two years into my explorations of the spiritual heart, I came to realize that there exists within us a realm of experience in which love as well as happiness, joy, and clarity are present, but which is inadequately described by all these words.

The ancient yogis called this realm—our "true" nature—*sat-chit-ananda* (pure being, consciousness and bliss).

The ancient tantrics had many names for it, including *spanda*—the joyful vibration of the mystical experience, the realization that all being is interconnected, indeed, one and the same, stemming from the same source, *shakti.*

Some more recent directions of spirituality call it the *zero potential*—the state of origin of all experiences, where everything is possible.

For myself, this state always expressed itself in the perception of almost indescribable beauty. I remember once, in the course of such an experience, being lost in the ecstasy of marveling at the beauty of a crushed beverage can lying on the street for at least half an hour.

Mystics of all times have told us that, seen from a perspective of spiritual clarity, all is well, everything that unfolds in our world is a perfect expression of the Divine. I would like to add to that: Not only is everything well, but even more, it is *beautiful* beyond measure, if we can but see it through unclouded eyes. That is why, incidentally, I've chosen the motto "Explore the Beauty of Existence" for my seminar business offering transformational retreats.

Why do most of us not experience this realm of love, joy and beauty all the time, but only catch a glimpse of it from time to time, like fleeting visitors to our actual home?

The ancient yogi Patanjali—author of the approximately 2000-year-old text of the Yoga Sutra—found a simple answer for this: it is our thoughts and judgments, the *choosing currents* of consciousness (*citta-vritti*), which pull us out of our inner center and obscure the state of happiness and inner peace that is always present within us.

Anthony de Mello, a modern twentieth-century sage and one of the great inspirations for my early spiritual explorations, had a clear idea about all of that, too:

To achieve the state of true happiness, he said, we must essentially just drop our judgments about what we want and don't want—we must change our evaluations of needs into preferences. Then, quite automatically, we will act out of happiness—out of love.

That sounds quite simple, doesn't it? Well, yes, but as we all know, it being simple does not necessarily mean it's easy.

In other books of this series, I describe in detail how we can work with our solar plexus and throat chakra to approach this ideal. After all, even in the blissful states described above, our judgmental mind continues to function—it is simply no longer in the role of ruler over how we feel about life. In this volume, however, we want to explore the direct route—straight to the heart of the matter, so to speak.

For about twenty-five years now I have been working with the chakras. In this work, I'm mostly using the so-called *shat chakra* or six chakra concept as described by tantric yoga. Essentially, these energetic structures are gateways helping us to describe and assess to what extent we are in harmony and in our power in all areas of our lives.

In the first volume of the Chakra Series, *The Power of Sankalpa,* on the solar plexus chakra, this meant to consider how we can consciously work with the power of our desires and create the life we want—how we can let our light shine.

In the second book of the series, *Be You to the Max,* on the throat chakra, it meant to explore how you can fully allow yourself to be yourself—to move into spontaneous, inspired action and expression.

And in the third, *Walking the Path of the Mystics,* on the third eye and crown chakras the focus was on transcending the concepts of "good" and "bad" and entering the realm beyond—or behind—the apparent world.

What, then, is the book you are now holding in your hands about? I've already mentioned it briefly: It's, most of all, about *beauty.* In the end, opening our hearts means opening ourselves to the beauty of all being. The more we can do that, the closer we come to the ideal of tantric spirituality: to be in a permanent state of infatuation, of amazement, of clear and loving perception with all creation—a state of ultimate connectedness.

Imagine how your life would change if, with every step you take, you could feel the earth kissing your feet and moaning with pleasure. Does that sound interesting? All right then, let's dive in!

Atma namaste.

Puerto de la Cruz, Spain, March 27, 2023

PART ONE

Exploration

Getting to Know the Spiritual Heart

"What your heart thinks great is great. The soul's emphasis is always right."

—RALPH WALDO EMERSON, SPIRITUAL LAWS

LOVE, JOY, INNER PEACE

THE HEART SHAPE IS ONE OF THE MOST INSTANTLY RECOGNIZABLE SYMBOLS IN MODERN HUMANITY. USED WORLDWIDE, IT STANDS FOR A WEALTH OF POSITIVE EMOTIONS. IN A SPIRITUAL SENSE, IT IS ALSO WHERE OUR INNER FEMININE AND MASCULINE MEET.

The Heart Symbol signifies, among other things, balance

Image Source: Getty Signature/pick-uppath

Chapter 1

Love—What Is That, Actually?

Love is a term that we are all familiar with. However, like "God" or "Freedom," it often remains rather abstract. For many of us, love has been fixed in our subconscious programming as an ideal, or even as an imperative. Such imprints, however well-intentioned they may have been originally, often result in making it more difficult for us to access the actual field of love. In this chapter, we will discuss what forms love can take, and what benefits a love-based practice may hold in store for us.

Love—what is that, actually? Have you ever taken the time to consider this question? If you haven't—I haven't, either, for a long time—I suggest you pause for a moment now to think about what love means to you and how it is and has been present in your life so far.

To say this here already: In the following chapters, you will encounter a number of little introspective impulses that will allow you to gain more clarity on some themes in your life that are relevant to unfolding the heart. Maybe you'd like to keep a notebook and a pen at hand while you are reading this book, in case you want to write something down.

So, let's talk about love. You have probably already noticed that in our culture we use the word love for quite different things.

However, love is always connected to some form of relationship—be it the relationship to ourselves, to partners, to friends and family, to animals, plants or even to more abstract things like a hobby or an ideal.

If we want to put it in as simple a way as possible, we could say that love is a heightened form of affection and connection.

Love and suffering are often close siblings, especially when unhealthy forms of attachment show up in those relationships—just think of addictions or co-dependency—or, likewise, if love becomes consciously or unconsciously conditional.

When we're unveiling and looking at the core beliefs from childhood that are most deeply rooted in our subconscious, ideas like "Love has to be earned," "I'm not lovable," "I have to sacrifice myself to prove my love," and the like are among the most common internalized beliefs. This seems logical, since for a toddler, the need to be loved by parents or caregivers must be a matter of immediate survival—physically and emotionally.

Many people see unconditional love as an ideal to work toward. This is true in a certain way. In all of my transformational retreats, forgiveness and developing a non-judgmental view of the world are important components and help participants to see themselves and their world with more clarity and compassion.

On the other hand, the socially embedded ideals of love that most of us are taught in childhood are usually not helpful, as they are easily misunderstood.

For example, the ideals on being a loving person I was taught as a child in the context of my partly Christian schooling rarely produced in me a sense of spaciousness, but rather one of constriction and presumed guilt. There was always some sort of underlying message in it, that seemed to say: You have to love everyone in the way we tell you in order to do it *right*. And if you can't do that, something is wrong. God won't be pleased. And so on.

Even if many modern societies nowadays offer their members a largely secular, legally liberated framework for authentic living, this fact is only slowly seeping into the subconscious, both that of ourselves as individuals and that of our culture as a whole. This is because old imprints of consciousness often need generations of consciously different thinking to completely detach themselves from the collective belief patterns.

Religions and governments, collectives and other power structures have always understood very well how to reinterpret the concept of love for their own purposes. The ideal of the martyr, for example, which has been widespread in Christianity since Roman times, bears witness to this. It was considered "cool", we could say, to be killed in order to prove one's love and loyalty to some religion rather than renounce one's beliefs.

During the big wave of nation-state founding in the eighteenth and nineteenth centuries, national anthems, national flags, and even founding myths were created—probably at least in part with the aim of strengthening identification with the state, loyalty, and "love" for the fatherland or motherland.

This was certainly good for motivational purposes, especially when such a structure needed or wanted to send soldiers into battle.

Prior to that, loyalties were probably organized on a smaller scale and in many places were focused primarily on the family or the village.

Why am I talking about these things here, in an exploration of heart energy and love? I'm drawing your attention to this because it means that most of us, simply by virtue of our social affiliation, are conditioned with a more or less strong set of beliefs, mostly only subconscious, that tell us: I *must* love.

This belief—similar to the infamous "love must be earned" pattern—may in some cases even effectively prevent us from expressing love in an authentic way. You'll hear more about releasing those blocks in Chapter 3.

Before we move on to this chapter's exercise, in which we will undertake a first expedition into heart energy, I'd like to take a moment to consider the different forms in which love can commonly appear.

The ancient Greek philosophers, for example, distinguished six forms of love: love of family (*storge*), friendly love (*philia*), romantic love (*eros*), self-love (*philautia*), hospitality (*xenia*), and *agape*, love of the Divine.

In Buddhism we find the term *metta*, loving kindness or compassion.

In classical yoga, *bhakti*, the devotional love for a master or for the Divine itself, was and in some cases still is, of great importance.

On Hawai'i, there is the concept of *aloha*, which also focuses on love and connection and which we will discuss in more depth in Chapter 9.

In my personal experience, love first and foremost permits us to really become aware of the object of consciousness we are directing our love towards—to open up and really be there, to *connect*.

Love has the inherent potential to transcend boundaries in a very real sense—especially the boundaries within ourselves that our thoughts and patterns have built up and that often make it difficult for us to be fully with the world and yet remain calmly centered within ourselves.

Of those among my personal meditation experiences in which the energy of love was the prevalent theme, I remember one thing above all: a sense of being touched by the almost indescribably intense beauty of the world and its beings. From this sense of beauty, wonder and amazement at the miracle that we ourselves are, and at the miracles around us, came the other aspects of heart energy that we most often hear about: joy, kindness, compassion, love.

When we can see the beauty that forms part of the essence of everything, it is hard not to love. And when we truly love something or someone, we also become able to perceive their inherent beauty.

So, this book will be about love, joy and happiness—but most of all, it is about opening our hearts to the true beauty of all being.

At the end of each chapter, in addition to the supporting meditation exercise, you will find some questions for self-inquiry (*svadhyaya*). These are meant to offer you a space for integration, as well as providing some ideas and impulses for further work with the themes presented in this book.

Exercise 1: I Love You.

This exercise is probably the most advanced and powerful meditation you'll find in the entire book, although it may seem very simple at first—and it is in fact simple once you find the mindset needed to access it.

It's a bit like those shifting pictures you sometimes find in exhibitions of visual illusions—it's the same image, but you can see, for example, a young woman or an old woman in it, depending on how you "tune" your perception. Even though it's advanced, I'd like to introduce it here, at the very beginning of our exploring the energy of the heart. In that way, if you like, you can practice it every now and then in your daily life while you are integrating the insights I share in this book.

In Chapter 10, you will find a slightly different version of this practice again, for integration, and also to allow you to feel into how working with heart chakra energy has changed you.

You'll see that it's quite easy and only takes a few seconds to do once you've gained a little bit of practice. In tantric yoga, such frequently repeated micro-meditations are considered at least as valuable as longer exercises.

For this exercise, you will need an object, ideally one that you can easily hold in your hand. For example, a pen, a book, or a stick of incense. Place it within easy reach.

If you don't have any suitable object handy, you can also do the exercise with one of your hands, preferably the non-dominant one.

To practice any of the exercises in this book, you can either read their description first and then start the meditation using a timer, or simply follow the instructions as you read the text. Although this is not a classical approach to meditation, I've found this method to be surprisingly effective,

> providing most of the benefits contained of the techniques in the most immediate way possible.

Sit comfortably and keep your spine erect. If you're sitting in a chair, make sure you can feel your sit bones and that the soles of your feet are resting firmly on the floor. You may need to move slightly toward the front edge of the chair to achieve this.

Close your eyes for a moment. Notice the flow of your natural breath.

Ask yourself, "How am I present right now?"

Notice everything that shows up in your body and mind in response to this question, and in general. Try not to judge. Focus on what feels good, without suppressing any unpleasant sensations that may be present as well. Just allow it all to be there.

Open your eyes and pick up the object you've chosen. Feel it and look at it from all sides, notice its texture, its weight, and its shape. Smell it. You may want to lick it. Then hold it in front of you so that you can look at it comfortably and with a gentle gaze.

Begin to say to the object: "I love you". You can do this out loud, murmuring softly, or in your head. You may even want to call the object by name. For example, "Pencil, I love you."

Repeat the phrase while looking at the object. Notice mindfully if your perception changes, and if so, in what way.

Continue in this way for a few minutes. Then, let go of the object, close your eyes, and observe your breath for a few moments.

> "I love you" is a very powerful mantra. If you like, try this technique today with some other things you encounter in your daily life. If you stick with it for a while, you may find that over time your perception changes, that you perceive things differently, with more detail and clarity, and that you feel more connected to the world.

Self-Study Questions for Chapter 1

Which of the six ancient Greek forms of love (family, friendship, partnership/Eros, self-love, hospitality, and love of God) are most present in your life right now?

For each of the above forms of love, recall a situation from your life when you felt that quality. How do the six experiences differ?

YAM

YAM IS CONSIDERED THE SEED SYLLABLE FOR THE HEART CHAKRA - A SONIC ACCESS POINT TO ITS POWERFUL ENERGY. THE SYMBOL OF THE HEART IS A STAR MADE OF TWO OVERLAPPING TRIANGLES, SHOWING ITS SIGNIFICANCE AS THE MEETING POINT OF DESCENDING AND ASCENDING ENERGIES.

The Heart Chakra Symbol according to Indian tradition
Image Source: Getty/svelby. Created using Canva Pro.

Chapter 2

The Heart Chakra and Love

In both the West and the East, we often locate our capacity for love in the heart. In this chapter, we'll talk about the nature of the chakras and how they shape our experiences in life. Chakra work can help us become more present with ourselves and our world—and this helps us to make those encounters more and more loving. At the end of the chapter you'll find a mantra meditation that uses the tantric seed syllable of the heart chakra. Love has much to do with our perception. We can train this through meditation and alignment.

After accompanying me through the explorations presented in the last chapter, I hope you have gained a bit more clarity on what love, as the primary quality of the heart chakra, means to you personally and in what forms it can manifest. In this chapter, I would like to tell you a little bit about the concept of chakras and why working with these ancient tantric energy centers can have such a positive impact on our lives.

For me, the chakras are the foundation of my own spiritual path, and I can't think of a better map for personal and spiritual development. Thanks to my work with this form of energetics, I would consider myself freer, happier, and more successful today than I have ever been in my life. I'd say I'm probably healthier, too.

The term *chakra* comes from Sanskrit and—literally translated—simply means "wheel". In some of my other books you can find a lot of information about where the concept came from and how it developed into what it is today. Since we're going to be working primarily with heart energy here, I don't want to burden you with too much theory, but rather focus on practical experience. However, I would still like to share with you some of the basics before we dive deeper.

The chakra model that I am using here originally comes from the tantric paths of the Indian subcontinent, although the Incas, Hawaiians, Egyptians, Chinese and other cultures have also known about these energy centers.

Today, the chakras are a tool often used in Western energy work to better understand our state of mind and life issues, as well as to address blockages and problems as directly as possible.

Chakras are often depicted as energy vortices in the midline of the body or spine. However, as with so much in yoga, the location in the body is merely a tool to help us better access these energy qualities.

Physical locations can serve as doorways, as it were, or controls for something that is happening all over the body and distributed throughout all layers of the aura.

There are potentially an infinite number of chakras that can be worked with, such as organ chakras or space chakras.

As you know, here we want to focus on one in particular: the heart chakra, also called *anahata*—the chakra of the unstruck sound. Viewed from the bottom up, it is the fourth chakra in the commonly used seven-chakra system—right in the middle between the lower (incarnating) and upper (excarnating) centers. It is the center of symmetry, so to speak, where our more material and worldly aspects are in balance with our more divine and spiritual parts. Ultimately, at the core of our heart chakra lies the potential of unconditional acceptance of ourselves and what is within us.

It is no coincidence that in many cultures the heart is also considered the seat of our Soul, our Higher Self, or the Divine Spark.

All chakras are subtle portals between that subtle part of ourselves and its physical expression in the material world. Put simply, they bring the contents of our aura layers into our direct experience.

It is not difficult to see that the heart, as the "seat of the soul," plays a central part in this. But it would also be a mistake to assume that love, as a quality of the heart chakra, cannot be present and felt in all the other chakras as well.

Each chakra, if you will, holds all the others within itself, giving its own unique flavor to their specific qualities. In Chapter 8 we will explore more of this inner interconnectedness between our worlds of experience.

Working with the chakras is directly related to our relationships. Relationships with ourselves, with others, with nature, with the divine. This brings us back to the concept of love—because yesterday we saw that love is a way of perceiving relationships. We can confidently say that the entire practice of tantric meditation is about relationship.

Incidentally, yoga nidra and all physical yoga styles are also tantric paths. By working with our relationship to what seems to be separate from us, we find ourselves in oneness, in the experience of how we are all part of the same great cosmic vibration. As you may know, one possible translation of the word Tantra is "web" or "fabric".

This book addresses a small but central part of this comprehensive relationship work and cultivation: the actual perception of the fact that we are connected to everything. Working with the heart chakra can help us to experience this connectedness more and more and to find freedom in it—the freedom to love.

This not only makes it easier for us to heal our relationship with the Divine and to awaken from the fog of unconsciousness. Above all, it holds the chance to sustainably change our lives and what we do, find and experience for the best of ourselves and the beings around us.

The following chapters will center on creating more mindfulness and connection with ourselves and others, and how we can use this to find more quality of life and more joy in our very concrete daily lives.

Exercise 2: YAM Mantra Meditation

In the early days of tantric chakra research, the ancient yogi's primary way of working with this concept was through sound.

Each of the major chakras was assigned a seed syllable that could be used to directly address and harmonize it. This was called a bija mantra

The Bija mantra for the heart chakra is YAM. Here, we will use it as a meditation object for a small mantra practice. This will help us to feel our way more and more into the topic of this exploration.

Sit with your spine erect and close your eyes. The soles of your feet should have good contact with the floor. If you slide forward a little on the chair, you can probably also feel your sit bones.

Notice how you maintain your upright posture, and at the same time relax all the muscles that you don't directly need to stay this way. This may include your legs, abdomen, jaw, and shoulders.

Notice how present you are. How is your breath flowing and where do you feel it most?

With the next exhalation, begin to sound YAM very gently. You can either extend the sound to include the entire exhalation, or you can sound several of the seed syllables in a row, like YAM YAM YAM YAM YAM...

Try both and stick with whatever feels better at the moment. The extended YAM tends to feel more relaxing for an evening practice, while the quick sequence of sounds tends to energize you.

Keep your voice very gentle and let the sound ride on the breath. Heart energy tends to be gentle and quiet.

Once you find your note, stay with it for the rest of the exercise. Notice everything that arises in you during the exercise—bodily sensations, spontaneous thoughts, images—but try to just observe it all, let it pass.

Continue doing this for a few more minutes.

Then release the mantra. Be aware of the flow of your breath. Be conscious of the sounds around you. Deepen your breathing and open your eyes.

An easy way to get a better sense of what effect any practice has on you is the following: Say "I love you" to some object you see after you finished your practice, and notice how this changes your perception. You may find that meditating before doing this intensifies the effect further.

Bija mantras are very powerful spiritual tools to work with. Other important Bijas are, for example, LAM for grounding, and HAM for freeing your authentic expression.

Self-Study Questions for Chapter 2

Have you ever worked with your chakras before? What were the results of that work? What is your relationship to the chakras?

Do you feel loved in your life? What experiences do you base your answer on?

DEAR SUPREME SELF!

I thank you for guiding me at all times in my thoughts, words and actions to fulfill our common cosmic plan in the best possible way. I love to trust myself, for I know that we are One.

Morning Prayer
Inspired by Huna-Shamanism

Chapter 3

Joy as a Beacon

Every day we make thousands of decisions in our lives, big and small. When we want to put love at the center of our lives, it is often not easy at first. This inner paradigm shift can be made smoother and more flowing by using the feeling of joy to guide our decisions. In our culture, however, love is often archetypically associated with sacrifice, bondage, and suffering. So, let's take a look at what often prevents us from connecting love with joy and what you can do to dissolve these blocks. In this chapter's meditation, we will explore some positive power phrases and learn how to use them as spiritual accelerators.

Over the previous two chapters, we have seen that love can come into our lives in many forms, and that working with the chakras can help us to bring all areas of our lives into harmony with each other and with our world. We have also seen that the qualities of heart energy—love, joy, inner peace and bliss—can be present in all the chakras before we learned about the seed syllable of the heart, YAM.

So far, so good. But how do we concretely fill our lives more and more with heart energy—indeed, how do we even approach the state of deep love and spontaneous presence that some of the ancient tantrics tell us is the result of centering in the heart? How do we know what to do to follow our life plan as directly and with as few detours as possible?

One key to this may be found in the quality of unconditional acceptance. Ultimately, happiness and joy are our natural state of being. In recent decades, it has even been proven by science that happiness does not need to have anything to do with our external life circumstances and our physical state of being.

Obviously, it's a little easier to feel happy if we don't have to fight every day to fulfill our basic needs like food or freedom, and if our bodies are more or less healthy and pain-free.

On the other hand, happiness is an internal state, and this means, it can be experienced at any given moment, no matter the circumstances. At least in theory. But we all know that, sometimes, outer circumstances can be near perfect, and we are still not experiencing happiness. So, what's happening there?

What prevents us from accessing this inner state which forms the core of our being, are our mental *conditions for what* we need to be happy. By this, I do not mean to feel good, or comfortable. That is something else again and it may well require certain external circumstances that fit our preferences. But we can choose to be happy! Often it is only learned and mostly unconscious patterns that tell us: "Until I achieved this, I will not be happy!"

Or, "As long as this or that condition exists in my life, I cannot be happy."

Or something like, "I am not worthy of being happy, in fact I am not even *allowed* to be happy (for instance, because my family didn't seem to be happy either when I was little, and subconsciously I don't want to break the 'rules' of my clan)". This is one of the particularly treacherous unconscious beliefs.

In general, the ideas that are embedded in us before the age of three are the most complex to work on. And because these patterns are formed based on the child's personal perceptions, even misunderstandings or situations that might be considered completely trivial or irrelevant from an adult perspective can lead to the formation of counterproductive beliefs. We will look at these mental structures in more detail further into the book.

One of the great gifts that heart energy can bring to our experience of life is the unconditionality that comes from knowing at our true core that everything is good. And when I say "everything," I mean everything. Even that which we may not rationally consider desirable, even that which we may fight against. Of course, I'm not saying that we should leave everything in our lives and in the world as it is.In my book, The Power of Sankalpa, I explain in detail why it is helpful to work consciously with our ability to make decisions and take action.

On the other hand, truly inspired action is only possible when we are at peace with ourselves and our world. And this peace, this unconditional acceptance and appreciation of all that IS, is the one quality of our hearts that most of us need more of.

That doesn't mean that we have to agree with everything. It simply means to remain aware that, from a higher perspective, everything is indeed good. And then to act in whatever way feels right. For we cannot *not act*.

From this relative unconditionality, we can actually become free to act inspired, because in this state we can be sure that we will most likely be able to accept whatever consequences result from our action.

The more we meditate and connect with our *kundalini*—the creative force within us—the less we have to think about what might be the most inspired and loving decision at any given moment—we just know. That is what I call inspired action.

However, very few of us start out with such a good connection to our intuitive guidance. As for myself, even after years of doing this work, there are still times when I am faced with a decision and do not immediately find clarity within myself. Usually this happens when it is either simply not important, because all alternatives seem equally desirable, or when one of the unconscious beliefs we just talked about is interfering.

So how can we follow our heart in a situation where the inspired impulses are too clouded to be distinguished from those of our patterns, beliefs, and our reasoning mind?

The aspect of heart energy that is most readily apparent to most of us is joy. If you are unsure of which path to take, follow the one that brings you the most joy. That's right, you heard me, joy!

Now, if you're saying, "But then maybe I won't ever file my tax return and I'll go to jail one day," or something like that, you're right. The heart is not interested in such trivialities, although of course there is the joy of a job well done.

But this is where its two most important helpers come in: our brains and our guts. Of course, we should not completely ignore either when it comes to following our hearts. Especially when you're just starting out.

Your intellect helps you anticipate the consequences of your actions in the future. Your gut, on the other hand, includes all the aspects of your decision that might somehow affect your well-being.

However, both can be overly dominated by fear, especially if old patterns in the subconscious still have a lot of power and emotional charge.

Ideally, we'll find a *Yes* in all three of these centers—then the course of action is pretty clear, but in that case you probably wouldn't even be asking yourself the question. If your head or gut is objecting to something that your heart would love to do, first ask yourself what might lie behind the objection. To do that, you might consider the following:

Is the negative consequence or failure you may be afraid of certain and real? Or is this just about expanding your comfort zone?

What's the worst thing that could happen? Would you be able to deal with it?

Is what you want to do in your best interest and that of your world?

What are the beliefs within you that make you feel insecure?

Is there an alternative that would give you just as much pleasure, but would be more compatible with the rational considerations of your head and the feelings of your gut?

In the specific example of the tax return that I just mentioned, we can assume with a high degree of certainty that we will receive a reminder or further problems if we do not file it. So I usually decide to do it on time, not least because it gives me the satisfaction of having crossed something rather unpleasant off my to-do list. So I am actually still on the path of joy with that as well.

When I quit my job as a manager in a big company a few years ago to dedicate myself to teaching yoga, I was able to realize that all the worries that had prevented me from taking this step for years had little substance, that they were primarily driven by beliefs that no longer needed to be valid for me. In this case, it was more than worth it for me to follow the joy.

Allow me to summarize: Heart-based decision making is based on unconditional acceptance of whatever happens. We can approach this state through meditation. Most of us are not yet in this state, or at least not all the time.

Therefore, it is helpful to let the feeling of joy guide our decisions. This ensures that you are not acting against the desires of your heart and your true nature.

There is a common belief that we cannot do exclusively the things that bring us joy, that we would then make too little effort, have too little success, that we would miss out on important things.

I do not agree. Even a great deal of effort can bring us a lot of fun and joy and may even feel completely effortless if it is done in accordance with our soul plan. So dare to follow your joy. Your heart will thank you.

Exercise 3: Heart Qualities

In this exercise, we are going to explore some positive power phrases that can be used to release and strengthen the energy of the heart. The main focus will be to feel the qualities of the spiritual heart more clearly from different angles and to find out in which areas you feel resonance or perhaps resistance.

> Resonance and resistance are two sides of the same coin. Both mean that there are emotionally charged contents within your subconscious that are reacting to the trigger that shows up. As such, they're equally valid indicators helping us to better see our shadows—the parts of ourselves that are so close that they're difficult to recognize, even though they influence our reactions, emotions and our general well-being strongly.

Sit with your spine straight and close your eyes. Notice how you are in the present moment. Observe how your breath flows. Where in your body do you feel it most?

Now bring your attention to your feet, knees, hips, your entire abdomen, your entire belly, your chest. Take special note of the space in and around the chest.

Keep your attention in the heart area as you hear some different words and phrases that I will offer you to feel into.

Notice whatever arises within you in response.

If you feel particular joy, agreement or resistance somewhere, take note of it.

Expansion.

I allow the love of my heart to heal everything in me and in my world.

Warmth.

I am a living expression of universal love.

Light.

Each day I plant seeds of love and joy in my life.

Action.

I am truth and love.

Power.

I recognize the perfection of all life and action.

Soul.

I am infallibly guided by my soul.

Breath.

My body is an contributing part of the earth,

a material expression of my multidimensional true nature.

Mother.

Father.

Siblings.

Connectedness.

Forgiveness.

Friends.

Liberation.

Community.

Truth.

Unity.

Freedom.

Gratitude.

Rest in the expansive space in and around your chest.

Notice how your breath is flowing now. Be fully present. How are you here, now? Then open your eyes again and be fully awake. Stretch and move a little, feel your body.

Well, how did that feel? Try to remember to which of the phrases you felt resonance or resistance. Either way, it just means that there is something in you that makes this aspect resonate, and that it is worth looking at more closely. You may also want to write something down.

If you would like to go deeper into one of these energetic qualities in your own practice, there are several ways to do so:

Like the seed syllable YAM we looked at yesterday, each of these statements can be used as a mantra meditation object. To do this, simply repeat the phrase on the breath, bringing your attention back to the mantra whenever your thoughts wander.

You can also use a phrase as the object of an analytical meditation. In this case, you set a timer and spend a certain amount of time just thinking about the subject, preferably without repeating a thought or argument in the same form more than once.

Another thing you can do is what I call an emotional meditation. This involves standing in front of a mirror, looking into the eyes of your reflection, and saying to yourself:

When I hear the phrase (or the word) ..., I feel....

Listen carefully within yourself and express whatever comes up as it comes.

There are still more ways to work with these phrases. You could go into almost unlimited depth with each and every one of the exercises we'll explore together here.

Self-Study Questions for Chapter 3

When you hear that you can actually just follow joy in your life: How does that feel to you?

Can you imagine unconditionally accepting and appreciating everything in your life, including all your past and future feelings, thoughts, words and actions? What would that be like? Is there anything you would do differently?

What would you do if you didn't need to earn money to live, and all your basic needs were taken care of for nothing?

Chapter 4

Self-Love

Can we fully accept and love ourselves, with all our rough edges, with all our strengths and weaknesses, with all our desires and needs, with all our feelings, thoughts, words and actions? Any attempt at outward love will remain essentially an empty shell until we have achieved this. Major stumbling blocks on the path to unconditional self-love are our inner critic and deep-seated family or social beliefs. These want to protect us from apparent danger. But that doesn't make them any less harmful. In this chapter, we will look at how we can energetically discharge such inner stumbling blocks and transform them into supportive structures.

We saw in the last chapter that unconditional acceptance of ourselves and the world around us is one of the most important gifts hidden in our heart center—a shortcut to more love, freedom and inner peace. We also discussed the ways in which we can allow our heart to guide our actions and how joy is an indicator that we are on the right path.

Let's come back to love, which is probably the most well-known manifestation of heart energy. How do we bring more love into our lives? Unconditional acceptance of reality and using joy as a guide is a good start, as we saw in the last chapter. But that still leaves us short of the deep beauty, intensity, and connectedness that characterizes the mystical love of the fully opened heart center.

The 13th century Sufi poet *Rumi* wrote:

"Your heart ist the size of an ocean. Go find yourself in its hidden depths."

What is it that keeps us from experiencing this love, this ocean-deep immensity of joy, all the time? What can we let go of, so that the armor that many of us wear around our hearts in one form or another can finally soften and melt away completely?

In this chapter, we will be looking at another key to the heart chakra: self-love and its main adversary, the inner critic.

Why is self-love so important? And it is important, perhaps for many of us the most important skill on the path to opening our hearts wide to life and the world!

For a long time I struggled to fully understand this point. After all, we are often culturally conditioned to believe that we already have more than enough self-love—

read: *selfishness*—and that we should be more concerned with loving other beings more. Self-love is equated in this view with "thinking only of oneself at the expense of others".

Undoubtedly, what I would describe as "unhealthy selfishness" has done a lot of damage throughout history. And indeed, destructive behaviors are also based on self-love—the desire of a person or being to satisfy their own basic needs, such as safety, food, and well-being.

However, the fundamental fallacy here would be to conclude that we can solve this by focusing more on projecting love and compassion outward and reducing the love and appreciation we give to ourselves. This is because destructive actions are not based on too much self-love, but on misguided strategies to meet our needs, on old unconscious imprints (this is what we call *samskara*s in yoga), and generally on a clouded mind that can no longer clearly perceive the impulses of the other energy centers and the body.

You can think of it that way: Basically, the mechanisms that make it difficult for us to express the love of the heart work the same way in all directions. Inwardly and outwardly. So we could actually start anywhere, outside or inside, and end up with the same result.

The reason I want to focus on self-love first is that this is usually where we find most of our shadows—things within us that we are only half aware of or even not aware of at all. This is because we all possess, since childhood, an *inner critic*—an entity that constantly judges everything we think, feel, do, and don't do. The inner critic wants to prevent us from doing something wrong. Its motivation is ultimately the fear of not fitting in, of being rejected, of being punished, or of being blamed.

This entity—which roughly, but not exactly, corresponds to Sigmund Freud's *superego*—is controlled by age-old beliefs and patterns, most of which have been solidified in our early childhood. It goes without saying that these things usually have little or no objective validity for us as adults. Nevertheless, they continue to have an unconscious effect unless we can consciously lead them to a resolution.

To summarize: The inner critic is an entity that also arises out of self-love and wants to protect us from problems. However, because it is controlled by old, unconscious patterns that were formed when we were babies, it is usually unable to assess the situation objectively and ends up going way beyond the goal of supporting us in our plans. Therefore, when we do not behave according to its demands, it acts as a block, reducing our self-love instead of increasing it.

The inner critic is a mental structure that draws its power from emotionally charged memories, especially from childhood. In my experience, it is the most powerful force that separates us from our heart's impulses, even when it superficially wants to do everything "right.

In order to move into more inner freedom and love, we can try to discharge the emotional charges of the underlying patterns by using techniques such as yoga nidra, forgiveness work, or quantum healing, and thus enable the inner critic to become more and more attuned to the actual circumstances instead of just repeating old reaction patterns. I go into this in detail in the second volume of the Chakra Series.

Here, however, in keeping with the heart quality of simplicity, I would like to introduce you to another, even simpler approach that you can use immediately and without much effort.

Since, as we have just seen, the inner critic is a mental structure, you can also talk to it in a mental way. Because it is a part of you, it loves you and wants to help you.

So, the first step is to fully accept it, as we saw in the last chapter. To step out of the struggle, so to speak. This is not the same as believing everything it tells you. But it does free up the stuck energy and makes it more accessible for conscious intervention—after all, there was a good reason for us to establish the patterns stored in the inner critic as babies—we were simply doing what we thought would ensure our survival. And this can and should be appreciated.

Once we've taken a step back from this internal conflict, we can use a technique called *Cognitive Reframing*.

Cognitive Reframing means, in essence, mentally examining the issue from all sides. This counteracts the inner critic's main tool for controlling your actions: narrowing your perspective. For, as already mentioned, it is primarily the clouding of the mind by overly dominant, often spiraling thought activity that prevents you from clearly perceiving the impulses of your heart.

So just look at what the inner critic is telling you from every possible point of view. Ask yourself these questions:

Is it absolutely true? Can you know it's true?

How would someone else see it?

What's the worst thing that could happen? How likely is it to happen?

How would you feel if it were someone else who did whatever you're criticizing yourself for?

How would you feel if you let go of this self-criticism completely, if it weren't there at all? How would you act?

And so on. You'll find that self-critical thoughts will always want to interject themselves into these reflections like spiraling structures. When this happens, simply don't follow them, but continue to explore alternative points of view without evaluating them against each other.

Try not to use the word "but" in these thoughts, as it has a strong power-sapping energy. The more you practice this, the faster your inner critic will understand that its view is not the only valid one—and the faster you will find your way back to inner peace and your ability to act. In the next chapter, we will go deeper into the subject of self-love and self-acceptance.

Exercise 4: Mirror Meditation

For this exercise, I invite you to stand or sit in front of a mirror or use a hand mirror to help you. You may want to pause the meditation until you are ready.

> If you don't have a mirror handy, just imagine your reflection in the mirror. All the exercises in this book are meant to be adapted in any way that fits your current needs and surroundings.

When you are ready, close your eyes for a moment and notice how you are there now. How does your breath flow now?

Then open your eyes again and gently look into the eyes of your reflection. What do you see? Always keep part of your attention on your breath while gazing at yourself, letting it flow as freely as possible.

Whenever you notice that you are holding or controlling the breath in any way, consciously let go of the control and then say to yourself: "Thank you. I love you." Continue like this. Notice the breath, let go of any control that you might sense, and say "Thank you, I love you." Do this for a few more minutes.

Then let go of the exercise. What do you see in front of yourself in the mirror now? Close your eyes and breathe. How are you present now, how do you feel?

Self-Study Questions for Chapter 4

If I asked you if you love yourself unconditionally, how would you answer? And why?

How often do you criticize yourself for something, and for what kind of things? How often do you criticize others, and for what?

Chapter 5

The Good Within

From an early age, most of us have learned to want to improve ourselves, and even to feel that we have to improve ourselves. Often, we lose the sense that we are already perfect—without having to first learn and without having to improve ourselves. Similarly, when it comes to our bodies, our brains are evolutionarily conditioned to be more aware of those things that are not functioning optimally. For example, pain, stiffness, or discomfort. The ninety-nine percent of our bodies that are actually functioning in perfect alignment and health tend to be forgotten, or at least not very present most of the time. In this chapter, we will look at how to connect with the fundamental goodness within us.

Are you letting your inner light shine as brightly as it could? Let's face it: for almost all of us, there is significant room for improvement in that. As we saw yesterday, one of the reasons for this is the existence of the inner critic, which makes it difficult for us to perceive the impulses of the soul in the heart clearly and to follow them spontaneously and trustingly.

The inner critic, this "criticism and evaluation machine" of our mind, is as powerful as it is because our entire social system is designed to train and strengthen it, to tell us what is right and what is wrong according to the social, school, or family consensus, and to influence us to believe in it.

These moral structures may work differently today than they did in the past, but they remain as strong as ever. In essence, from early childhood we are more or less subtly conditioned to want to conform to the expectations of some group. This may be, as I said, our family, the school system, society as a whole, or any number of subcultures, such as that of religion.

The ancient philosophy of Tantra, on the other hand, tells us that any form of morality and structure is unnecessary if we can be alive, present and centered in the heart. For the heart is not interested in fixed structures, but in the immediacy of the present moment.

Any form of rules and morality is ultimately based on the assumption that we would not or could not act "well" on our own. As such, they are an expression of our brain's tendency to focus on, and remember more readily, what is not good.

This makes some evolutionary sense, of course, since we all want to avoid danger, but it has become something rather counterproductive in the context of our current, largely very safe world.

If I ask you what your body feels like right now, the first parts of your anatomy that come to mind will probably be where there is tension, pain, or other discomfort.

I am proposing that we slowly begin to move this tendency of our consciousness toward the skill of giving more weight to what is positive and good in us than to what may not be going so well at the moment. Without ignoring or suppressing anything, of course—just placing it in a larger context. For it is only when we fully embrace the fundamental goodness of our nature and our bodies that we can also grow into that unconditionality that we have been talking about a few times in the last chapters.

Using the body as an example, consider this: The very fact that you are here and alive right now proves that ninety-nine point nine-nine something percent of your body is functioning in perfect harmony and health. Otherwise, you would be dead.

Of course, it can be quite uncomfortable when the remaining zero point zero zero something percent gets out of balance, but still that fundamental fact remains and can be the basis for immense gratitude once we are truly aware of it. And out of this gratitude, even those areas of us that are causing less well-being at the moment can always start to heal. It is also uncontested by medicine that our self-healing powers are very strong, and that stress is one of the main causes of the immune system not doing its job properly. In the light of this realization, it seems only logical that it can only be good for us if we let go of destructive criticism—because, as we all know from our own experience, it ultimately creates inner stress.

Stress, by the way, is considered by the ancient Taoists to be the shadow side of the heart—the antithesis of the love, joy and happiness we feel when the energy of this center is allowed to flow freely.

Can you trust yourself unconditionally? Can you believe that you, as part of the earth, are unconditionally good and deserve only the best? Feel that for a moment...

If you now feel resistance to this idea, ask yourself what it would be like if it were true.

How would it feel? How would it feel if you were not judged or evaluated by anyone for who you are and what you do? If not only your own inner critic would let you off the hook, but all other people and society as well? What would you do with this freedom? Do you feel worthy of it? Let this idea work within you.

Exercise 5: Focusing on Pleasant Physical Sensations

In this practice, we are going to learn how to perceive pleasant sensations in the body and how to anchor them to counteract any tension or discomfort.

Sit comfortably, close your eyes and be fully present.

How is your breath flowing in your body right now? Is there anything else you can do to make yourself more comfortable for the next few minutes? If there is, do it now, as mindfully as you can.

Now bring your full attention to your feet. Notice everything you can feel there right now. Pay particular attention to pleasant sensations.

If something unpleasant arises, notice it too, without dwelling on it or giving it more importance than the other sensations. This could be the contact of your soles on the ground, the space between your toes, the blood pulsating in your veins...

If this feels right, thank your feet for carrying you through life as reliably as they can. You may want to tell them, "I love you".

Now do the same with your ankles. Send mindfulness, gratitude and love into your ankles.

Move up to your lower legs and shins and do the same.

Observe everything, don't hold on to anything.

Then, notice the knees, all sensations that are there right now, especially the pleasant ones.

Thank the knees for allowing you to take steps, to move, to stretch, to kneel.

Be aware of your thighs, the muscles, the strength that is in them. Thank your thighs. How much can you appreciate them?

Notice your pelvis, your hips, your lower abdomen, your genitals. Be fully present in this area, what do you feel there now? Focus on what is pleasant, let unpleasant things come and go, don't repress anything, don't hold on to anything. Mindfulness, gratitude, love and appreciation.

Now bring your focus to the abdomen, to all the organs there, the intestines, the kidneys, the bladder, the stomach, the spleen, the liver.

Thank your organs for keeping you alive day after day, processing food, taking in what is important, eliminating what is no longer needed. Notice everything. Where does the belly feel particularly good?

Then the diaphragm and chest. The lungs taking in oxygen and expelling what is no longer needed. The physical heart, tirelessly pumping blood through the body, transporting vital substances, and creating a powerful electromagnetic field around you. The ribs, which hold it all together and protect it. How does this area feel right now? Give it your full attention, gratitude and love.

Move your awareness up to your throat, where the food pipe, windpipe, blood vessels and nerve pathways pass through, where the vocal chords that allow you to sing and speak are located, as well as the larynx that allows you to swallow. The throat also is the place where the connections between the brain and the rest of the body pass through, the spinal nerves.

Notice everything, don't cling to anything. Mindfulness, gratitude, love.

The entire head, containing the brain and the sensory organs that allow you to perceive and enjoy the world. The hair, if you have any, which protects you from the sun. Mindfulness, gratitude, love. Thank you, head!

All of your skin, which separates your physical body from the outside world and gives you the sensual experience of touch. Thank you, skin! I love you.

All the nerves, blood vessels, muscles, the bones of the skeleton that allow you to walk upright, to move at all, especially the spine.

The body in its totality. Notice everything, don't cling to anything. Awareness, gratitude, love.

Notice your emotions, the vibrations that make life so much more colorful and intense, that guide and direct you. Be aware of how you feel now. Mindfulness, gratitude, love.

Turn to your thoughts, the conscious mind that allows you to understand things logically, to form and understand words, to see inner and outer images, and to be creative. Mindfulness, gratitude, love. What would you be without your thoughts? They are such powerful helpers.

Breathe freely and be fully present. How are you present now? How does your body vibrate? What emotions are flowing through your being?

Finally, in your own time, open your eyes and end the exercise. Namaste.

Self-Study Questions for Chapter 5

How often do you feel gratitude in your daily life? What are you grateful for? If you like, write down some things and feel deeply into their essence and meaning for you.

How do you see your relationship to your body? If you were to meet it as a separate being, what do you think it would say to you? What would be your own message to your body?

Chapter 6

Life is Relationship

The ancient tantric philosophers tell us that everything is connected to everything else. Even our bodies, our earthly shells, can only function because each of our cells is constantly interacting with a multitude of others, forming organs, and controlling life processes. On a larger scale, we are all part of greater organisms—family, friends, society, and Gaia, the world. We are connected to the world around us in a very real way. As sentient beings, we are—you might say—a conscious part of the world, the eyes and ears of the Earth, as our own eyes and ears can be considered part of us. Recognizing this can assist us in accessing the field of love.

The British-American philosopher Alan Watts once compared our relationship as living beings with the

Earth to that of the fruit of an apple tree with the tree that produced it. The apple tree apples, the earth humanizes, is roughly how he put it.

In Christian mythology, as you may know, there is the archetypal image of being cast out of paradise, "the fall from grace."

One interpretation of this image is that at some point, as more self-aware beings, we began to feel separate from nature and from each other—that is, through knowledge and self-knowledge, we lost our "innocence," so to speak. Whether this should be seen as something negative or positive is a matter of perspective. The fact remains that this story can essentially be interpreted as a movement from unity to duality.

Of course, we are in interesting territory here, as Christian theologians have certainly been debating this topic in a hundred different ways for a very long time. Personally, I'm not that interested in theology.

Nevertheless, it is an exciting story, and it can be inspiring to think about the value of innocence as a quality of the heart and what it means in your personal worldview.

Let's come back to the tantric worldview, which is the main resource this book draws on. Here we consider this movement into duality not as something negative, but as probably the only way for the divine to experience itself—to play, one might say. Lord Shiva, who symbolizes consciousness in tantric symbolism, dances with Shakti

—the personification of matter, the vibration of all that is experiential in itself.

Here's the thing: because we are all essentially expressions of the same power, the Divine that has split itself into parts to play with itself, we are, of course, all deeply connected.

When the mystics tell us things like "all is one" or "even the greatest thing is contained in the smallest," they are saying just that: everything in our perceptible reality is interpenetrating.

But we have obviously chosen, at the level of the soul, not to be aware of this—because if we were, the game would be over.

Now, of course, this is a rather philosophical statement—energetically, I am now speaking more from the upper chakras than from the heart.

I just want to illustrate that connectedness is a real and tangible quality of all being—not something we have to create through some kind of practice.

The more clear and present we become, the more we can perceive this connectedness. And yet it has always been there. When we look deeply enough into it, we are no longer an individual having an experience in the world—we are the world itself. We are not living our lives —we are life, as even the Bible tells us, if we are willing to assume that maybe Jesus was talking about himself as a human being when he said that.

We do not live on the earth—we are an integral part of it with our physical existence in a very real sense.

As we saw in Chapter 2, all experience is ultimately relationship. And specifically, as I have just argued, a relationship between you and yourself, in which you face yourself in the form of an infinitely diverse world.

That's a bit of a provocative idea, isn't it? But I'm not trying to sell you a solipsistic worldview, which would be the idea that the world and everyone else exists only in your consciousness—the consciousness of what I call the "small" ego. Rather, I am suggesting that you see your ego, and even your soul, your High Self, as a wave or current in the infinite sea of consciousness. Even if this is no more than a hypothesis in our everyday consciousness—at most supported by an occasional mystical experience of oneness—it is still a way of looking at things that can make it tremendously easier for you to feel the underlying connectedness of everything. Love then comes as a natural consequence.

If you like, try the following in your daily life:

Whenever you meet a person, imagine that you are meeting yourself in that other form. Or, if it feels easier for you, imagine that you are meeting the Divine in another form, just coming to teach you or to play with you.

This is a very powerful technique for opening the heart. I can promise you that once you've done this for a while, you will not be the same person you were before.

Exercise 6: Lovingkindness Meditation

This exercise is about *metta*, loving kindness, and has been inspired by Buddhist meditation.

Sit comfortably with your spine erect and close your eyes. Notice how you are there now and how your breath moves the body. I will now suggest some things you can say to yourself and others in your life during the exercise.

> If any of these don't feel good, modify them to suit your needs. For example, you can always say, "I open myself to the possibility that..." or "I imagine what it would be like...". This is also a highly effective way to de-block your mental powers if at some point you don't find a solution for a problem. Ask yourself: "If there were a solution to my problem, what might it be?" Often, this slight rephrasing unblocks the subconscious and allows it to come up with more creative ideas.

Let an image of yourself appear in your mind's eye. Say to yourself, in your mind or in a whisper, "I now choose to love myself. I now choose to accept myself. I choose now to accept myself fully. May I be happy. May I be free. May I be healthy."

Now, visualize a person or other being in your inner space for whom you feel deep affection. Say to them: "May you be happy. May you be free. May you be healthy."

Do the same with someone you are more neutral towards, for example a chance encounter or a casual acquaintance.

Say to them: "May you be happy. May you be free. May you be healthy."

Now bring into your mind a person towards whom you have rather negative feelings, about whom something bothers you or who has hurt you. Say to them, "May you be happy. May you be free. May you be healthy."

Repeat these sentences with all the people or beings that come to your mind.

"May you be happy. May you be free. May you be healthy."

Continue doing this for another few minutes.

Then detach yourself from the exercise again. Notice how you are there now. Notice how Life breathes you. Now open your eyes and be fully awake.

Thank you for being a part of this and for allowing your heart's energy to shine forth ever more brightly. You are important. Namaste.

> Consider for a moment how much importance do you give yourself, right now? How powerful do you feel? Just by

virtue of belonging to the human species, you are an immensely powerful animal. Let that sink in for a moment. Can you believe that? How does that feel? How does it influence the sense of responsibility you feel to the beings around you?

Lovingkindness meditation is one of the cornerstones of many Buddhist paths. From Buddhism also comes the ideal of the Bodhisattva, the intention to achieve awakening not only for oneself but to help liberate all beings.

Self-Study Questions for Chapter 6

How connected do you usually feel to the people in your life? How do you notice that?

When you hear that all the beings you meet are divine teachers, how does that feel to you? Are there examples in your life where you can feel that? Are there people for whom you can't imagine it at all, where you feel resistance to even considering them as teachers? If so, why?

Chapter 7

How to Be Connected

Whether with ourselves, other people, things, or life itself, love always unfolds in relationship. Our ability to feel love is directly related to our ability to relate. In this chapter, we will explore the four human attachment styles from psychology and see how they influence our personal capacity to love. You'll also get some ideas on how to cultivate a secure attachment style with yourself, strengthening not only your ability to connect more genuinely with partners and friends, but also your ability to love your life itself.

In the last chapter we saw that as spiritual beings we are fundamentally connected to everything and everyone in our world. In fact, from a higher perspective, we can say that we are one with our world. At the same time, we have seen that our apparent separateness is a direct result of the divine drive to be playful, a desire for encounter and commonality. In this chapter, we want to look at how we can make these encounters more beautiful on the level of feeling separate—that is, the level on which we usually live our lives, and what knots we can untie on this level in order to really enter into relationship with more authenticity and love.

Now this is going to get a bit theoretical at first. In the end, however, you will see that it becomes quite simple.

The first relationship we have in our lives is with our caregivers as a small child. Normally, in modern nuclear families, these are primarily mother and father, and perhaps siblings or other relatives.

Science tells us that between our birth and the age of three, our brains operate primarily in what is called the delta frequency band—a range that adults reach only during deep sleep. It is not surprising, then, that much of the most essential and deepest "basic programming" of our experience is anchored in our subconscious at this age. This includes our basic conditioning about relationships and connecting with others.

Let me say up front that nothing about this is unchangeable. Relationship skills can be acquired at any time in life—they're just more or less pre-programmed in all of us.

An equally important observation is to recognize that no one is "to blame" for programming that may be less than optimal or even dysfunctional later in life. Even if the caregivers were acting in a psychologically impeccable manner and the circumstances were favorable, it is the child's subjective experience that determines the form in which these patterns are solidified. Even events that seem harmless from an objective point of view can create unhelpful core beliefs if they are resonating with the child and are perhaps further reinforced by a misunderstanding.

I believe that the nature of our basic patterns is to some extent determined before we are born—conditioned by the experiences and processes our soul wants to go through and possible ancestral imprints we want to release.

Of course, this applies to all unconscious imprints or samskaras, not just the ability to relate. But that is what I want to talk about here—specifically, attachment styles, the way we experience connection with partners, family, friends, and other people in general.

In attachment theory, there are four basic attachment styles that determine our ability to bond—that is, how well we connect with others and with ourselves, and how well we feel about ourselves in the process. According to research, about sixty percent of people display what is called a *secure attachment style.*

What this essentially means is that they tend to be comfortable on their own as well as in the company of other people, and can be available to their partners without either feeling pressured or becoming overly clingy. In terms of childhood experiences, it is assumed that these people have experienced sufficient availability of their caregivers and, at the same time, sufficient freedom to make their own experiences, knowing that the caregiver will be there when needed.

In attachment theory, we find the image of an attachment figure as a perceived *secure base* and *safe haven*.

This means that having such an experience imprinted in our subconscious during childhood greatly increases the likelihood that we will find it easier to access this sense of security in later relationships with partners, friends, and groups, as we have developed the ability to take on these roles for ourselves as well as for the others with whom we relate.

For the remaining forty percent or so of people, it is assumed that there was a perceived lack—whether objectively present or just experienced internally. This results in what are called insecure attachment styles, which, by the way, can later manifest quite selectively in certain areas of our lives and not in others.

If the child experiences that the attachment figures are somehow not sufficiently available in its perception —i.e. this safe haven and stable base is not there in a subjectively sufficient manner, then according to attachment theory the so-called *avoidant attachment style* can develop.

This may happen, for instance, if a child repeatedly experiences that no one responds to its crying, again in a subjectively sufficient way, which may vary depending on the child's personality and other basic programming.

A person who develops this attachment style is likely to become very autonomous and independent due to the experience of having to care for themselves, but, simply put, without additional learning processes, will have difficulty allowing closeness and feeling properly in contact—simply because the basic pattern was not created in this form, or was created only to a limited extent. Typically, these are people who can easily switch from being with others to being alone, but have more difficulty doing the opposite.

The second type of insecure attachment is called *anxious attachment*. It seems more likely to occur when the attachment figures in the child's experience were sometimes available and sometimes not. The person learns that intensifying contact efforts sometimes leads to success and becomes, simply put, more clinging. This type of anxious attachment also tends to produce a heightened sensitivity to any sign that the relationship is not going well enough.

The third insecure attachment style, sometimes called *chaotic* or *anxious-avoidant*, is a mixture of the previous two. It is thought to occur when the child subjectively or genuinely perceives a caregiver as a danger. The desire to seek refuge with the caregiver is then directly in conflict with the desire to be safe from the caregiver, creating a kind of oscillation between the two states.

Why am I telling you this here, in a book on heart energy? It is very simple. If you are affected by such insecure attachment styles in certain areas of your life, it can be very helpful to become aware of them. Since, as mentioned, these mechanisms are solidified early in life and thus usually function unconsciously, we can rarely perceive them directly without help, at most through their impact in everyday life—usually in the form of a lack of stability in partnerships, friendships, and other social contexts. However, if we become more aware of them, we can turn to possible solutions.

There are many books and approaches for developing a secure attachment style in adults. My personal favorite approach is—you may have guessed it—self-love. If we can manage to be a safe haven and stable base for ourselves, and help our inner child understand this in a positive way, then we don't need to avoid connecting (because we're afraid of being disappointed and think others won't be there for us when we need them anyway) or become overly attached (because we think we're dependent on other people).

So, we can safely say that self-love and nurturing contact with ourselves is a good first step. And that's what you are practicing if you choose to work with the exercises presented in this book .

Of course, this has been an extremely short presentation of a rather complex topic. However, I am sure that even this basic knowledge will be very helpful to you as you continue to liberate your heart energy in connection with others. If you would like to delve deeper into the subject on your own, there are many resources available on the Internet and in bookstores, as well as online tests that you can use to determine your own attachment style.

Exercise 7: Deepening Connection

This exercise is a meditation that offers you some positive impulses designed to expand your ability to connect in a loving way with yourself and the world around you.

Sit up straight and close your eyes. Notice how your breath is flowing right now. Can you release control still a little more?

Now consciously bring your attention to the area of your heart.

Dwell in the vast inner space of your spiritual heart. Notice everything that arises.

Sound YAM, the seed syllable of the heart, inwardly or with your voice a few times.

Yamyamyamyam....

On the following page, you will be seeing some statements. Notice carefully what feelings or images arise in you as you go through them.

Notice everything, do not cling to anything.

I am free.

I trust myself and I trust life.

I am completely lovable.

I walk the path of love within and without.

I am comfortable in my body.

I deserve the best.

I choose to live healthy and fulfilling relationships.

My heart is open to love and deeply fulfilling relation-
ships of all kinds.

It is safe for me to express love.

It is easy for me to accept love, from myself and from
others.

I am complete, I have all that I need.

I bless all beings in my life with love.

My contacts with others and the world are close,
loving, nurturing and marked by mutual respect

I let my inner light shine.

I am full of self-love and inner peace.

I am filled with gratitude.

I am in harmony with all beings.

I acknowledge the divine in myself and in all beings.

Peace flows through me, all pressure dissolves.

I radiate love with my entire being.

*I radiate love in all my thoughts, feelings, words, and
actions.*

I forgive myself and all others unconditionally.

It is easy and simple.

I live in ease, connection, and joy.

Pause. Notice how your breath is flowing now. How do
you feel?

Then let go of the meditation. Open your eyes and be
fully awake. Namaste.

If you noticed particular approval or resistance to any of
the phrases I presented to you in this meditation, you may
want to write them down and feel into their meaning for
you a little bit deeper. One easy way to do that is taking
a page and jotting down everything that comes to mind
when you consider the concept expressed by the phrase.
Approval, doubt, dislike, whatever comes up. This will help

> you gain an ever clearer picture of yourself and your conscious and subconscious patterns.

If you resonate with affirmation work, you will find a list of more positive thoughts related to the heart chakra in the Annex to this book.

Self-Study Questions for Chapter 7

Feel into which attachment style you mostly display in the important relationships in your life (partnership, friends, family, society). What is it? Are you satisfied with how it affects your interactions? If you like, you can find free tests on the Internet to help you determine your attachment style.

On a scale of 1-10, how satisfied are you with your relationships right now? Why?

Basic Chakra Symbols and Bija Mantras According
to Indian Tradition

Image Source: Getty/selimcan. Created using Canva Pro.

Chapter 8

The Links Between the Chakras

All beings and situations we encounter in our daily lives hold a mirror up to us. Whenever that mirror presents itself in a less than pleasant way, we often tend to project blame or negativity outward. The more we can allow our heart energy to flow freely, the easier it becomes to see these people and situations as valuable teachers and to develop gratitude for them. The resonances that bring such mirrors into our lives are radiated through the individual chakras. In this chapter, we will look at their energies as well as their shadows.

The influence of the heart chakra on the other chakras may be considered a relatively advanced topic.

Throughout the last few chapters of this book, I have been sharing about the importance of our subconscious patterns and imprints, and their significance in determining what kind of experiences we will encounter in our lives, how we will relate to ourselves and others, and how we will emotionally interpret external events.

From an energetic point of view, these imprints are stored as condensations in our aura layers and send out a certain energy signature or resonance through the chakras into the world of experience. Thus, our subconscious imprints are not only responsible for our reactions to what we encounter in the outside world—they also function as attractors to draw into our lives the kinds of things, situations, and people that fit that resonance.

In a very real sense, every living being we encounter holds up a mirror to us, showing us our own energetic interior. This applies not only to human encounters, but also to all the other things and situations we encounter on a daily basis.

If what we see in the mirror happens to be of a less than pleasant nature, it is tempting to project blame or negativity outward onto the external circumstance or influence that is triggering these feelings in us. But of course it is not helpful to blame the mirror for those of our resonances that it reflects back to us. If you change the mirror, it will still reflect the same thing in front of it if it has not changed.

The more we can get our heart energy to flow unimpeded, the easier it becomes to see all kinds of interactions and situations as valuable teachers and to develop deep gratitude for the mirrors they hold up to us.

This enables us to see ourselves more clearly and to release old blockages that may still be preventing us from living a life of maximum joy.

I've said this before, but just to be sure, the fact that another being shows us our own shadows does not mean that we have to blame ourselves if we have an unpleasant encounter—after all, these resonances work unconsciously. Nor does it mean that we should just allow anything to happen to us.

In fact, we just act as we normally would. However, by being aware that we are facing a mirror, it tends to be easier for us to find an appropriate form of response than if we get lost in external projections.

Allow me to elaborate a bit on how this process of creation works. As mentioned earlier, the resonances that draw these mirrors into our lives are radiated through the individual chakras—and by connecting them to the heart chakra we can enrich all the resonances we send out with love. This works because love is not limited to the heart chakra—we can feel it in each one of our chakras and use it to heal any old hurts and unhealthy imprints.

To give you a clearer picture of how this can work, in this chapter's exercise I am going to walk you through a brief overview of the main themes and interrelationships of the different chakras.

It is important to note that this is only one possible model for you to work with. Energetically, you create your own reality, so you can also create your own access portals to your experience and subconscious imprints.

The chakra model is relatively common and is used by many people in a similar way. This makes it relatively easy to tune into the collective field and thus access something that cannot be so clearly defined. It is more like a diffuse overall experience of the constantly changing wave in the universal sea of consciousness of our true nature.

So, we can say that the chakras are a purely practical and interchangeable tool to work with, nothing more.

Basically, we can visualize the arrangement of the seven known major chakras in many different ways, of which I will mention the three best known here:

The first is that of a tree growing from the top down, with its roots in the sky. This is the classic incarnation process, the descent from subtlety into matter, embodiment, personification.

Swiss psychologist Carl Gustav Jung is reported to have said that hardly any human being was fully incarnated in this world.

After analyzing my own meditation experience, I can now agree with this view, even though I would never have believed it at the beginning of my involvement with yoga. Back then, I actually thought I was incarnated enough and wanted to go up—into the clarity and beauty of mystical experience. And I did. But that's not all there is.

The upward movement I used to find so cool as a teenager is what the second view is about. It is the idea of the tree growing upward, with its roots in the earth, or—in the body—in the feet, the coccyx, and the pelvic floor. This is also reflected in the yogic view of the kundalini or shakti energy, which is seen at the base of the spine and, as it becomes more activated, slowly works its way up through the chakras or granthi—knots—until it reaches the crown chakra. This is the excarnation movement, the movement from the predominantly worldly oriented person to the spiritually awakened one.

You see, at first glance there appears to be a contradiction between the first and second views. The second either assumes that we are already fully incarnated and embodied and want to get out of it—or at least as fully incarnated as we want to be. Whereas the first tells us that we are actually not as fully there and alive as we would like to be. In any case, both agree that we need to unlock the longitudinal connection between the chakras in order to realize ourselves in our highest form.

The third view that I would like to present to you here also agrees with the others on this point. Here, however, we place the heart in the center, which is essentially at the intersection or strongest concentration of celestial and earthly or matter energy. The heart, as we have already seen, is also where our divine spark resides, our true nature, which ultimately pervades and renders insignificant all notions of heaven and earth, of above and below, of inside and outside.

From the energy of the heart, our being expands and solidifies in a constant cosmic breathing movement, oscillating between the subtle and ethereal and the earthly and vibrant.

The heart is the only chakra that has the power to penetrate and heal all the other centers without affecting their essence.

You can think of it this way: When we try to harmonize our lower chakras with more mental-spiritual, subtle techniques, the very vital, the sexual and the instinctual are often lost.

Many ways, religions, masters and students that relied or still rely on celibacy and abstinence to sublimate the sexual power into the higher chakras and went awry a bit in the process bear witness to this. It sometimes works, but in my experience this is almost always at the expense of true aliveness.

Meanwhile, pathways that focus primarily on working with the lower chakras, resolving trauma and imprints, and releasing sexual power often lose clarity and inspiration.

The heart sits at the center of all energies and has the potential to bring both extremes together to unite them into something harmonious. That is why it's crucial to base spiritual practices in the heart if we aim to unfold the powers awakened by meditation in a harmonious and compassionate way.

Exercise 8: Chakra Inventory

In this exercise I'm going to guide you through a little inventory of your chakras. This will help you to see into which areas of your life you might want to direct a little more of your heart energy.

Sit and be aware of your breath. How are you here now?

Close your eyes and bring your attention to the vertical midline of your body, on the inside of your spine.

Imagine the seven major chakras lined up along this central axis like a string of pearls.

Begin with the root chakra at the bottom of the pelvic floor and tailbone. This center represents our basic trust in life, our ability to process fear, and it is also the foundation of our courage to live, our ability to be fully alive.

How fully alive do you feel and could there be more? Stay in the pelvic floor area for a moment. If you like, say: Thank you. I love you.

The sacral chakra in our lower abdomen is related to sensual pleasure and joie de vivre, intuitively knowing where we want to go in life, and accepting ourselves as sexual beings.

How much do you enjoy your life? Stay in the lower abdomen area for a moment. Say if you like: Thank you. I love you.

The solar plexus chakra above the navel represents the solar power in us, courage, initiative and action. But it's also about digestion in the broadest sense—how we deal constructively with the things that come our way in life.

How powerful do you feel in your actions and how clear is the expression of your will? When others don't act the way you want them to, how relaxed and confident are you in accepting that? Stay in the navel and upper abdomen area for a moment. If you wish, say: Thank you. I love you.

I don't need to introduce the heart chakra in the chest area any further, we have been working with it intensively for the last few days.

How much spaciousness, acceptance and lightness can you feel here right now, how do you relate to yourself and your world? How is your inner critic doing right now?

Stay in the area of the rib cage for a moment. If you wish, say: Thank you. I love you.

Now move to the throat chakra in the area behind the larynx. This is where you can allow yourself to show yourself exactly as you are, to let your light shine without worrying about what other people think of you.

What is your voice like? How do you like to sing, speak, or otherwise express yourself creatively? How comfortable are you being heard? Do you like to say what you think or do you tend to hold back? Do you swallow things you don't like?

Stay in the throat area for a moment. Say: Thank you. I love you.

Move your awareness to the third eye between the eyebrows, also called the *ajna* chakra. This chakra centers on insight, clarity of any kind, and your ability to think as a rational being.

How lucid do you feel? Do you perceive your thoughts as helpful servants, or do they cloud your mind? How do you make decisions? Do you perceive subtle energies and intuition, or do you rely primarily on logic and evaluation?

Stay in the area of your eyes and forehead for a moment. Say: Thank you. I love you.

Now move up to the seventh chakra, which you can visualize just above your crown. This chakra has to do with knowing your own divine nature, trusting in higher guidance, mystical experiences, and realizing that you are more than your physical body.

How easy or difficult is it for you to imagine that you are an expression of the Divine, as perfect and vast as the entire universe? Stay in the area above the crown of your head for a moment. Say: Thank you. I love you.

Finally, be aware of all chakras at once, lined up like a string of pearls.

Then take one deep breath in and out. Open your eyes. Direct your awareness outward and be fully awake and present. Namaste.

Self-Study Questions for Chapter 8

Which of your chakras do you see as most in need of development at this time in your life? And why?

How easy is it for you to see the reflection of your conscious and unconscious inner life in external encounters? Can you think of situations in which you have felt this? Or are there occasions when it has been more difficult to accept this idea?

Chapter 9

Aloha—Heart Power in Hawai'i

"Ike pono mea" is a Hawaiian proverb that means: every-thing, everything is as it should be. If it doesn't seem that way, we are simply not seeing the whole picture—then what we need most is not change, but Ike, the right per-spective. Many meditation paths place great emphasis on non-judgment -an extremely valuable practice for devel-oping more heart energy. In this chapter we will talk about Aloha and how we can better integrate the principle of love and inner peace into our daily lives.

As we saw in the last chapter, the power of our heart chakra has the potential to positively influence the vibration of all the other chakras and their respective areas of life. We are now already quite deeply into our topic, and I hope that along the way you may have had

one or two moments that have given you not just a theoretical but an embodied sense of what this is all about.

We have already explored the subject from a number
of different perspectives. I would like to share one last
one here with you before tomorrow we talk about how
we can best integrate all of this into everyday life. For
that, we're heading to the middle of the Pacific Ocean.

In fact, when it comes to the embodiment of love, I
think it is very worthwhile for us to look at the example
of another culture that has studied this issue in great
depth: That of the islanders of Hawai'i, one of the most
isolated land masses on earth.

You have probably at some point heard the term
aloha, or perhaps even aloha spirit. Aloha is often used
as a greeting—aloha kakahiaka, for example, means good
morning—but it's much more than that.

Aloha embodies the essence of community and love.
It goes without saying that a culture that developed
some 1,500 kilometers from the nearest inhabited island
and over 3,000 kilometers from the nearest major land
mass has evolved its own world view.

Aloha is seen by many as the force that holds the
universe together, and the aloha spirit is even enshrined
in Hawaiian law as a mandate for public servants.

Here, however, I would like to introduce you not primarily to Aloha, but to two other qualities of the heart
that are part of Aloha and that I have come to know especially through my Hawaiian teachers: Fun and ease.

In several chapters of this book, we discussed some rather challenging aspects of the subject: Obstructive beliefs, cognitive reframing, the inner critic, relationship styles—that all sounds a bit like work, doesn't it? Kind of heavy, serious, actually. Yet, I don't think the essence of heart energy is serious in the least.

When we're in love, of course, we don't get serious either, but rather light and playful—at least if we're not too hindered by the above-mentioned beliefs. So let's end by diving into the ease and spaciousness that pure heart energy can offer us: the deep knowledge that we are only actors in this great cosmic play, and that we are here to have fun!

Do you allow yourself to have fun in life? If not, or not all the time, what might that feel like? Think about this for a moment...

How seriously do you take yourself and what happens to you in your life? And is there another way?

In the first chapters of this book, I talked about how unconditionality is one of the most important gifts a liberated heart force can give us. We can approach this unconditionality through the conscious practice of non-judgment and non-evaluation—and this also allows us to move away from the seriousness of life into a lightness that can actually be a lot of fun.

There is even a kind of side benefit to all of this: the more fun we have in and with life, the more we can be sure that we are on our souls' path, and the more our increasingly light resonances will attract people and events into our lives that are compatible with this basic attitude. So, no matter how you look at it, having more fun brings us many benefits.

But what if we ever experience something that we don't enjoy? We have talked about some of the things we can do in such a case over the past few days.

But the Hawaiians provide an even simpler solution: Aunty Mahealani, a wise woman from near Hilo who left her body in 2021, once told an interviewer what she was told to do when she was feeling unhappy as a child. Just sit on a rock, look out at the ocean, and come back when it's okay, the adults told her.

I think that's a very heart-based way of looking at things. Things don't always have to be as complicated as we like to make them. And that's what we can learn from the heart. Simplicity. Lightness. Spaciousness. Joy. Connection.

Ike pono mea is a saying that I also first heard from Kumu Mahealani. If we just look at things the right way, everything is in alignment—*Pono*.

In the shamanic path of Huna, Pono is often considered the highest vibrational energetic principle of Hawaiian spirituality, even more powerful than Aloha. This is because aloha still carries a kind of evaluation, namely that everything is good and lovable.

Pono, on the other hand, leaves out the judgment and essentially tells us the same thing that mystics of all cultures and times have always wanted to tell us in many different forms. Everything IS, perfect beyond any form of description and beyond even the possibility of imperfection. This knowledge is stored in our heart and is accessible from there.

Exercise 9: Fun

This practice is a thought meditation. The object of meditation is a specific subject.

Your only task will be to allow only thoughts, memories, and images to arise that are related to that subject. If you notice that you have become distracted by another thought, simply turn your attention back to the subject very gently and without judgment.

Sit comfortably and close your eyes. Be aware of your breath. How are you here now?

Now begin to think about what you enjoy most in your life, where you have had fun before and what fun means to you. What memories come to mind, how did you feel, what did you smell, taste, see, hear or feel?

Keep thinking about fun.

After 5 to 10 minutes, end the exercise.

Let go of your reflections and just be.

How are you here now? How is your breath flowing?

Try to feel the residual vibration of the space you have created. How do you feel about having fun now?

Open your eyes and be fully awake. Namaste.

Self-Study Questions for Chapter 9

How often in your life do you really have fun, and when?

If I tell you that you are here to have fun, what effect does that have on you? Does it feel liberating? Confining? Confusing? Or expanding?

Chapter 10

Joyful Amazement

When we perceive something with presence and mindfulness, love is the natural outcome. So if we want to invite more love into our lives, we don't have to add anything, we don't have to learn anything. All we have to do is let go of, or at least soften, our judgments and interpretations of how things should be. The aim of this exploration, however, is not merely to cultivate emotional love, but a lasting sense of sensual enchantment—the mystic's blissful delight in engaging with the world as a beloved. In this chapter, I will suggest some ways to bring this rapture and wonder at the miracle of yourself and the world more and more into your life.

Over the past nine chapters of this book, we have been working on examining the heart chakra and heart energy from different angles. You may have noticed that we've been approaching the subject primarily through the doorway of the mental—our thinking mind, our sixth chakra, the third eye. Of course, this is partly due to the format of this book—words are inherently intellectual and first have to be transmitted into a lived experience by the reader—, and also to the origins of my personal yoga path many years ago in Jnana Yoga, the yoga of understanding, which is part of the reason why I like this format. Analyzing things and making mental connections is relatively easy for me.

So, although there is also a kind of energetic transmission through the field within which we are all connected, at this moment I am communicating with you mainly through words and concepts. These words are addressed first to your rational mind, and only then do they trigger something in your experience. I bring this up because there are, of course, other ways of working with the heart energy that may be a little closer in nature and in the way they touch you to the essence of this very subtle and gentle power—the energy that we can feel in those moments when we have really come to our center.

Rumi did it through poetry. Certain fairy tales and inner images contain and channel a lot of heart energy. I myself am always very touched in the heart by visual art, especially nature and animal photography. Of course, nature itself can also be a gateway. A conscious walk by the sea or in the woods is one of the most heart-opening things you can offer yourself.

Meeting other people who are very centered in their hearts can be very opening. The Indian master Amma, for example, hugs people and in this way transmits her message.

In tantric massage, we use touch and connection with other people as an object of meditation.

In conscious dance, we can express emotions like love, joy, and connection without the detour of mental interpretation.

So you see, there are many paths. The love of the heart pervades them all.

As I mentioned at the beginning, for me the most tangible expression of heart energy is the perception of the immeasurable beauty of even the smallest thing we encounter in our lives. The wonder of it, the joyful trembling at the miracle of life. Because we live in the midst of miracles. Think about this for a moment.

Embodied heart energy has a very sensual quality to it, something deeply pleasurable. Spiritual heart energy feels expansive, open.

And at the core of the heart energy—well, that's where the mystery is, the actual experience of the fact that we are all connected, that we are all one. Everything else comes from that.

Right now there is a glass of water in front of me. As I focus my attention on it and try to really notice it, it becomes more and more beautiful. The curved line of its wall, its symmetry, its softly rounded edges. The deeper I immerse myself in it, the more grateful I become for its existence. Not only for the fact that it allows me to quench my thirst, but simply for its existence. For the people who were involved in its creation. From the sand miners to the merchants.

I caress its smooth surface. The deeper I go, the more I imagine that the glass enjoys my attention and appreciation as well, that it, as the ancient tantrics would say, nestles comfortably in my hand and moans with pleasure.

For this is what the Tantrics essentially tell us—everything has consciousness.

This worldview, by the way, is what in the West is referred to as *panpsychism*, and it is a very helpful working premise for tapping into our heart energy.

But let's not talk about it now. Because we are starting to get close to wrapping up.

How can you bring what you learned here into your daily life?

Each of the exercises we have done offers almost unlimited potential for going deeper. I suggest that to begin with, you focus mainly on the mini-practices—for example, you might resolve to say "I love you" to something or someone ten times a day, and then see how your perception changes. Of course, you can also just think the words.

Or every once in a while, when you meet someone, imagine that they are a perfect expression of the Divine.

Or you can get into the habit of looking into your own eyes every time you pass a reflective surface and say: "I love you. I see your beauty." An essential aspect of the energy of the heart is simplicity. You don't need anything complicated. It's all here.

The following exercise concludes the main part of this book. In the following chapters you will find some more in-depth impulses on how to integrate the work with the heart chakra and the development of more and more authenticity into your yoga practice, breath work and other forms of practice.

Exercise 10: Beauty, Love and Gratitude

Do you remember that I promised you in the first chapter that we would revisit the technique introduced in the "I Love You" meditation? You may even have practiced it from time to time over the past few days.

The following exercise is a continuation of that technique, offering the potential to drop you even deeper into connection with yourself and your world.

Sit upright and close your eyes for a moment. How are you here now?

How does Life breathe, *inspire* you in this very moment?

Be aware of your contact surface on the floor and on your sitting surface, perhaps the soles of your feet and your sit bones.

Relax your abdomen, shoulders, and jaw.

Then open your eyes and begin to look carefully at everything you see around you now. Focus on the beauty of things. If you like, say to each of the things you see around you, "I love you. I see your beauty. Thank you for existing."

Stand up and walk around the room, giving your appreciation to everything. While doing so, also remain aware that whatever love you give to the outside world, you are also giving to yourself at the exact same time, without having to do anything in return. Love is essentially directionless.

Continue with the practice. Go into more and more detail. You may notice things in the room that you haven't paid attention to in a long time.

Do this for a few more minutes. Maybe you'll want to use a timer.

Then sit down again and close your eyes. Notice how you are here now.

Open your eyes, stretch and move a bit and be fully awake.

> If you like, you could try this exercise with another person as well. That could also be silently in your head with a passerby on the street or the cashier at the supermarket. Alternatively, if you know someone who is also interested

in these things, you could even face each other in a partner meditation and do this together. Set a timer, each person says these power phrases to the other for a few minutes, and after each time you both feel into what this does to you.

The clearer you see something or someone, the easier it is to love them. This may (or may not, after all the work we've done here) seem counterintuitive at first glance, but it is also important to note that loving someone, for instance in a relationship, obviously does not mean staying with them if this clarity shows that the partnership does not reflect the highest vision of who you are anymore. The observation still holds true, since self-love needs to be the basis of all our other expressions of love, and self-love asks us to be authentic, in the first place. Namaste.

Self-Study Questions for Chapter 10

How do you feel right now in your heart space?

Has anything changed in relation to the qualities of heart energy in your everyday life since you've been doing this course? Can you find examples of this?

PART TWO

Deepening

Integrating Heart Energy in Life

"True genius without heart is a thing of naught—for not great understanding alone, nor imagination alone, nor both together, make genius—Love! Love! Love! that is the soul of genius."

—GOTTFRIED VON JAQUIN

MIRRORS

*EVERY ENCOUNTER IN OUR LIVES HOLDS A MIRROR
UP TO US, SHOWING US OUR SHADOWS, THE THINGS
WE CAN'T SEE ABOUT OURSELVES OF OUR OWN.
CAN YOU CONSIDER ALL BEINGS YOU MEET IN LIFE
AS DIVINE TEACHERS?*

Heart Energy shows up in all of our relationships -
with ourselves and others
Image Source: Getty Signature/gremlin

Chapter 11

The Heart Chakra in Physical Yoga

Asana is the Sanskrit term for physical yoga postures. In our contemporary culture, yoga is often reduced to the more physically oriented forms of this ancient path—although the word yoga itself simply means *connection* and was originally practiced primarily in the form of seated meditation. The blending with tantric elements then led to a desire to eliminate physical causes for the clouding of our minds, and as a result began to focus on health-promoting and detoxifying body postures and breathing techniques.

With the exception of the YAM mantra meditation at the very beginning, most of the exercises I have presented in this book have more to do with Western energetics and with *jnana yoga*—the yoga of knowledge—than with the more familiar *hatha yoga*.

In yogic literature, though, you will find many approaches that suggest "heart-opening" hatha yoga sequences and practices.

I don't want to go into too much detail here, but simply share with you some principles for incorporating any form of mindful body work into playing with heart energy—including but not limited to physical yoga, qigong, conscious dance, and many other ways of consciously engaging with the body.

As a yoga teacher, I find myself coming back to three aspects that I believe can be used as cornerstones of any physical practice:

1. Mindfulness,
2. Love, and
3. Freedom

All three of these principles are directly related to heart energy. When I sometimes hear about yoga teachers who get injured in practice (I know an orthopedic surgeon who actually specializes in treating such cases), it always reminds me how important it is to listen to ourselves and our bodies when we do anything.

I myself, after about fifteen years of intensive Hatha yoga practice, suffered a knee injury that took almost two years to heal. At the time, I too had fallen prey to the idea that, on a physical level, "it will work out" if we just practice often enough. Well, sometimes it does— and sometimes it doesn't.

In our society, we are typically conditioned to believe that we can stretch our limits by pushing against them over and over again. This is really very, very deeply ingrained in most of us. So deeply, in fact, that many students have difficulty understanding what I mean when I say that, interestingly, we can transform most effectively from the center of our comfort zone.

Indeed, many of our pursuits seem at first glance to support the theory that it is only by constantly testing our limits that we can truly grow.

Let's consider the example of weight lifting. I don't know what the fitness trainers at the gyms are currently saying is the best way to build strength. I haven't lifted weights for a long time.

In general, though, there seem to be two extremes here, that we only work with weights that are comfortable for us and stop training before we get some kind of exhaustion or even pain, or that we try to go to the limit, and maybe beyond. What seems clear is that the physical risk of either immediate or long-term damage tends to be higher with the second option than with the first.

It is also clear, however, that in either case we are at least giving our muscles an impulse, a sense that they are needed. In either case, over time we will be able to lift a little more weight comfortably or do more repetitions. By the way, it has been scientifically proven that the mere thought of exercising our muscles makes us stronger. In a lot of disciplines of modern fitness and wellness, including some forms of physical yoga, the comfort zone is sometimes looked down upon. But the ability to consciously anchor ourselves there can help us enormously in expanding it.

I do not want to say, however, that pushing the limits can't be fun sometimes. What I'm saying is that it is not about doing uncomfortable things until they become natural or comfortable. Instead, we want to consciously do pleasant things until our comfort zone naturally expands, and with it, our possibilities. This is a much more heart-based approach.

Now, you may think that's obvious. I think it should be. Then again, maybe you'll say that you enjoy feeling your limits and strain yourself, because it makes you feel good, because you feel like you are getting ahead.

That used to be my reason for putting undue stress on my knees for years, sitting cross-legged for hours doing exercises like the well-known "pigeon pose," which, in the case of rather inflexible hips, tends to twist the knees rather than "open" the hips.

If you already have fairly flexible hips, the pigeon pose may not be a problem for you, but it's still likely that you'll get more benefit from doing more things that strengthen and stabilize.

In short, heart energy in body practice means first and foremost taking ourselves and our bodies seriously and looking at them with loving mindfulness. If your body doesn't feel good after doing an exercise, don't take it as a sign that you're "not ready" or "can't do it," but as your body telling you to do something differently next time.

And if you listen to your body, adjust your practice, and try the more difficult thing again later, it may suddenly come naturally and without effort.

Mindfulness, love and freedom—this includes giving yourself permission to change things in any way that feels good to you. It means not believing in other people's structures, but mindfully looking at yourself and then acting on what you perceive.

Finally, here are some simple physical exercises you can do to support your heart energy:

1. Backbends. In yoga, backbends are generally considered rather heart-opening. You can do this very gently, sitting on a chair, preferably on the inhale. You can support the opening forward by gazing diagonally upward and opening your arms to the side or in a V-shape to the ceiling. I like to do this myself in the morning when I get up, sitting on the edge of the bed. You may want to sound YAM, as we did in the exercise for the second chapter.

2. Hand Exercises. In yoga, the hands are considered secondary chakras and functional organs of the heart. For example, you could interlock your fingers and gently stretch your hands in all directions. Or clap them. Or stretch them horizontally in front of you and alternately open and close the fingers. The second hand opens only when the first is closed. This also trains the coordination between the left and right hemispheres of the brain.

3. Shake. Shaking generally brings the entire body into vibration. Be sure to shake upwards rather than downwards, i.e. pay more attention to pushing off the earth than to shaking something off.
4. Raise and lower the arms. Raise on inhale, lower on exhale, preferably alternating between the front and sides. Try asymmetrical or chaotic movements.

Simplicity is one of the most important qualities of the heart-one that we can always return to.

Another important part of physical yoga is the science of breathing techniques. Since breathing and the heart are closely related, not only in location, we will discuss this in more detail in the next chapter.

Chapter 12

The Heart Chakra and the Breath

Your heart and lungs together inhabit the ribcage, the space in the upper half of the torso, and they are separated from the other organs by the diaphragm, our primary respiratory muscle. *Samkhya* philosophy, which is closely related to yoga, assigns the element of wind or air to the heart.

Also associated with the heart is the skin, one of our largest organs, which is also home to the sense of touch, through which we can feel the wind on our skin and enjoy the pleasures of touch and massage, among other things. Each of our breaths also massages our heart, which is directly connected to the diaphragm via the heart sac (pericardium).

You may have heard of heart rate variability (HRV). Simply put, HRV is an indicator of how much conscious and unconscious stress is present in the human body. It is based on the discovery that stress reduces the flexibility—or variability—of our heart rate. In a healthy, relaxed individual, the heart rate is constantly changing according to the needs of the body and its organs. One of the body processes that a relaxed heart adapts to is breathing. That is, the heartbeat will usually slow down a little on the out breath and speed up again on the in breath. When the sympathetic nervous system— our fight-or-flight mechanism—is overactive, it seems to override these natural fluctuations by keeping the heart rate up, or at least more constant.

This makes sense, of course, if—as some of our ancient ancestors may have had to do—you are preparing to run away from a cave bear in the immediate future. However, if you're just a little overworked all the time and worried about answering all your emails before you leave the office, it stands to reason that keeping your body in a state of subconscious alertness is not helpful.

Consequently, the HRV indicator can be used to measure the effect of relaxation and meditation exercises on your body, and also serve as a general indicator of health and immune system function. You may know that stress also reduces immune system responses by directing energy to the parts of the body that would be needed in case of fight or flight.

Why am I telling you this? It is for two reasons: First, you may find this information helpful if you want to go even deeper into heart chakra work. There are quite a few readily available biofeedback applications using HRV on the market today, if that is something you are interested in.

My main reason for mentioning HRV, however, is to illustrate that in a heart-based practice, it is more helpful and healthy to release the breath and thus the heart rate, rather than to control it.

Yoga teaching sometimes gives the impression that there are "better" and "worse" ways to breathe—that, for example, deeper and slower breaths are somehow better than fast and shallow ones. I have been practicing this for a long time, and there is some validity to this view in very specific situations.

For example, if we want to calm our nervous system, it is usually better to lengthen and deepen the out-breath, perhaps even to sound as we do so. On the other hand, if we want to be more awake and active, it is more helpful to focus on a full and perhaps slightly faster in-breath.

In deep meditation, the breath can become very shallow and almost imperceptible. There is even a name for this in yoga—*kevala kumbhaka.*

As we have seen above, however, the main point is to let the breath flow as freely as possible, so that it can adapt as naturally as possible to whatever is happening in our lives and in our bodies. There is another reason for this besides health. Both Breath Therapy and Breathwork demonstrate quite beautifully that most of the subconscious imprints and programming we've been looking at in the early chapters of this book show up in our bodies as specific breathing patterns. Just think of a situation where you were triggered. It will almost certainly have been accompanied by a constriction of your breathing.

In my own practice, I have found that liberation of the breath equals liberation of the mind. That's why, if our goal is liberation, inner freedom, it's so important to consciously work on freeing the breath from constrictions and patterns.

Sure, it can be useful from time to time to use certain breathing techniques, to join a breathwork chapter where you consciously breathe deeply and connected, and the body can also go into hyperventilation states—which, by reducing the thinking activity of the cerebrum, for example, allows us to dissolve old patterns very quickly and feel the energy flows in the body better.

But the main goal of any heart-based breathing practice should be to dissolve breathing patterns, not to create new ones. Only a free breath will allow your heart energy to flow into manifestation in a clear expression, largely untainted by patterns and imprints.

Therefore, the more control we can give up, the better. The more naturally we can work with the breath, the better. Again, letting go is a free ticket to happiness and freedom.

One of the easiest and most natural ways to practice with the breath is through chanting and sounding. In Taoist energy work, the tongue is also considered an organ of the heart, for example by Qigong master Mantak

Chia, with whom I've had the pleasure of learning on several occasions during his visits to Europe.

It is also simply fun to make our voice sound, if we can overcome possible negative imprints associated with it. Whether you can sing "well" or not is a minor consideration, obviously. In general, if you can speak, you can sing.

You might want to start singing outside, in nature, maybe near a waterfall if you feel uncomfortable being heard. Or at home in the shower. Find your own words and tunes. Maybe just humming. Use a Western or Eastern mantra. Or make up gibberish, syllables and words that have no apparent meaning to you. Sing with the trees or a bubbling mountain stream. Be creative.

Any expression of your voice helps not only your heart but also your throat chakra to unfold. Trust yourself. If you like to sing with others, find a *Kirtan* chanting circle near you.

A variation of working with the breath through the voice is mantra japa. In the yogic context, mantra japa refers to the repeated, mostly whispered, mumbled, or silent repetition of mantras in daily life.

All of the affirmations and power phrases mentioned in this book are excellent for this practice. In my book on Sankalpa, you can learn more about how to create and adapt such phrases for yourself and your life goals.

Choose a phrase (mantra means *tool of the mind*) and repeat it regularly. If you like, you can use a prayer chain, a Buddhist or Hindu mala, or a rosary. Traditionally, most mantras used for mantra japa come from Indian culture, such as:

Om Namah Shivaya.

Honoring Shiva, the source of consciousness, to the constant change of all being.

Om Parashaktiyai Namaha.

Honoring the vibration of the world we live in, to the Divine Mother, to our own essence as incarnate beings.

Lokah Samastah Sukhino Bhavantu.

May all beings live in well-being, peace and liberty.

Atma hridaye. Aham amrite. Amritam brahmani.

A Vedic heart mantra. Roughly translated: My soul is in the heart; meaning, I am one with the heart. I am the nectar of immortality. The nectar of immortality is one with the Divine.

But again, be creative. Pay attention to what suits you now. Other exciting mantras to experiment with may include:

YES.

I love myself and you.

Thank you.

Joy.

I am completely present.

I trust myself.

I love to trust myself.

I give thanks for my existence.

I love being here and having this experience.

Do not change mantras too often. It is best to stay with the same one for a few months to really feel its effect in depth. In the yogic and Buddhist traditions, we sometimes find minimal indications of the number of repetitions needed for optimal effectiveness of the mantra, usually depending on the number of syllables. These recommendations usually range from tens to hundreds of thousands. But don't let that scare you. Do whatever feels good to you. Experiment, and observe.

To conclude this chapter on breathing, I would like to discuss the second most common way we use our breath: talking.

The most common way, of course, is simply to take in oxygen quietly. But often we also talk to each other—yet another way of expressing our relationship with the world around us. We have worked with directed words a few times in this book, for example in the mirror exercise or the "I love you" exercise.

Some of the texts you'll find in this and the next chapter have been adapted from my throat chakra book, Be YOU to the Max, also published by Chakra-Atelier.

Since the way we speak and what we say is also very important for the expression of our heart energy, I have included and expanded these contents for this title in order to convey their importance for heart chakra work.

The Bible says, "In the beginning was the Word".

In a yogic context, it is OM that we speak of as the primordial sound, the primordial vibration of the universe.

The ancient Hawaiians knew that words were so powerful that they could be used to bend reality.

All spiritual traditions have their own texts or oral transmissions and stories that attempt to express and record the experiences of their founders and adepts.

Language and words are a central part of the human experience, one of the central pillars upon which our societies are built. Our thoughts are often expressed in the form of an inner dialog, in words. This book, too, consists of symbols on paper that are transformed into words and contexts through learned patterns in your mind, creating meaning and context.

When thoughts are expressed through sound, that is, when they create an externally audible vibration, then we are speaking—and others can hear, record, and respond to our thoughts.

What are you saying and how are you saying it? With this question you can easily determine how our heart energy is doing. This is done simply by becoming aware of how you speak in different situations.

Furthermore, how consciously do you choose your words? I'm always amazed at how many strange associations have seeped into our use of language. For example, when someone tells us something is "insanely good," we all know what they mean. But do we really want to invite madness into our lives, even if only subtly and unconsciously? Nothing to worry about, of course, but still an interesting area of practice.

In Ho'oponopono and Hawaiian shamanism we call this verbal hygiene, and fortunately it works the other way around as well. By choosing to talk about the things you want to feel more of in your life, you can help them materialize.

Can you remember what it feels like to talk to someone you trust one hundred percent, where you know you will be accepted for who you are? With whom you can be radically honest. Who may even make you feel loved.

You may find that in such an encounter your breathing flows more freely, your voice sounds different, and you use different words.

As I said before, I encourage you to experiment. And be attentive to how different situations affect you. This also helps you find out what nourishes you, how you can deepen your balance and enjoyment of life. In a very real way, any spiritual practice is an experimental science of life.

Chapter 13

Self-Analysis and Shadow-Work

Self-analysis is called *svadhyaya* in the yogic context and is considered one of the most important foundations of any spiritual development, along with steady practice (*tapas*) and faith (*Ishvara pranidhana*).

At the end of Chapters 1 through 10 of this book, I have included some questions that you can use to deepen your personal experience of heart energy.

In this final chapter, I would like to give you a few more hints on how to recognize more and more of yourself, and how to find the best questions to support this quest.

Often, finding the right questions is a large part of any desired solution. For the shadows that are anchored deepest in our subconscious are sometimes very, very hard to see—because they're so entrenched in our wiring, our "base programming," that we actually believe they are who we are, part of our personality, our ego's self-definition.

As we have discussed at length, all of us carry these shadows—or unconscious patterns—that were established in early childhood. I want to go a little deeper here, at the end of this book.

When I say "shadows" here, I don't mean something dark or "evil," but simply all those parts of ourselves that we can't really see—because they are in the shadows, perhaps repressed. Perhaps they are already so familiar that we cannot see them anymore, or they are simply not compatible with our beliefs about what is allowed to be and especially how we are allowed to be.

There is something very strange about these shadows. We usually only see their traces, their effects in our lives. Things that don't go our way. Unintentional hurts to others. Inner discomfort although we think we are doing everything "right" and in tune with ourselves. Resonances that draw things into our lives that we would never consciously want—or reject experiences and people that we actually long for. The old example of people who often end up with an incompatible partner of the same type is still a valid illustration of this process.

To change anything about a shadow—we might call it a blind spot—we first have to see what's in it. But that's about as difficult as figuring out where we're going in a car with no windows.

If we have excellent knowledge of the area, know exactly where we got in, and are paying close attention, we might have a chance. Still—a tricky task.

Fortunately, few of us live alone in a cave in the Himalayas, but in our beautiful human society. That is, we encounter dozens to hundreds of fellow human beings almost every day of our lives—all of whom hold up a mirror to us, as we saw in Chapter 8. In that chapter, I suggested that you focus on the chakra that holds the resonance that brought this encounter into your life.

Some of the primary chakra energies and areas of life experience you can work with are the following:

Root - Trust, abundance, and contentment

Sacral - Enjoyment, relating, and sexuality

Solar Plexus - Power, action, and motivation as well as digesting experiences

Heart - Unconditional love, joy, and presence

Throat - Authenticity, permission, and expression

Third Eye - Perception, worldview, and clarity

Crown - Connection to the Divine

Reconnecting the affected chakra with the unconditionality of the heart energy, you will find that this tends to make it easier for you to see the other person as an actual divine teacher who may have something important to tell you—if you manage to listen in the right way.

To support this process, it can be helpful to ask yourself the following questions whenever you find yourself in an uncomfortable, confusing, or otherwise intense situation:

What is it that this person can show me about myself?

What is it about this situation that I should not miss out on, what can I learn from it?

What about me comes to light in this encounter or life event that I don't otherwise perceive?

How are my automatic reaction patterns playing out, and am I comfortable with them?

Where do I know this feeling from? Are there any old memories coming up?

If I find something unpleasant in the other person's behavior, have I ever behaved that way toward myself or others?

If the situation tends to be positive for you, you may also ask yourself what the elements are that make the experience feel positive? What do you like about it? This will also tell you a lot about yourself.

> If the person supplying you a mirror to your resonances is reasonably mature in spiritual and human terms, you can also ask them for direct feedback, and simply talk about how the situation affects both of you, in order to gain more clarity about your shadows:
>
> *"What are your feelings about our interaction / relationship and what are your feelings about me?"*

Most people—incidentally, including your own inner child—respond well to open conversations. In the case of more aggressive conflicts, of course, it's more difficult and usually doesn't do much good, because the other person subconsciously wants to impose his or her own projections on you first and foremost.

In any case, you should be aware that all of us, no matter how "evolved" we believe ourselves to be, are always involuntarily projecting our inner selves onto others.

Therefore, the feedback you receive from others about you will ultimately tell you more about them than about yourself, and you should never unquestioningly accept the judgments it contains. However, by doing so, and especially by observing your own reactions to such external stimuli, you can begin to get a clearer picture of your shadows.

When you recognize such a shadow, you will probably find that it is more of a moment of revelation than an "Oh God, I'm so bad, I have to fix this right now" moment. Be loving to yourself, practice non-judgment, and change course gently and mindfully if that's what's needed.

Just think what would happen if you could actually see every human being and every animal you encounter today as a divine teacher who has come to you specifically to show you something and to accelerate your unfolding. What would that be like for you? What would change in your life?

With that question in your heart, I am going to leave you to discover for yourself. Let your light shine—for yourself and for all of us. *Namaste.*

ANNEX

Resources

Power Thoughts and Impulses

"You are the soul of the soul of the universe. And your name is love."

—RUMI, AFGHAN 13TH-CENTURY MYSTIC

Heart Chakra Affirmations

Below you will find a complete list of all the positive affirmations related to the heart chakra gathered in this book, plus some additional ones, each enriched with some thoughts, impulses, and explanations.

You could try reading some of these affirmations to yourself every morning in front of the mirror. Look into your eyes and smile to yourself. Also, have the courage to create your own intentions based on these inspirations. Allow yourself to be creative.

If you want to delve deeper into the work with affirmations and creative intentions, you can find a complete list of power thoughts for all seven chakras and their respective areas of life, as well as many other impulses and basic rules for formulating intentions and new states of being in my book, The Power of Sankalpa, and its accompanying audio course.

I collected these power phrases along my twenty-five year long practice and exploration of spirituality. Most of them are quite universal, and I encountered them in different places. Primary inspirations for my personal work with words were Louise Hay, Ulrich Dupree, Horst Krohne and all of my yoga teachers.

Action.

The heart is our primary organ of action and spontaneity. This is reflected in the fact that in yoga philosophy our hands are considered secondary heart chakras. How can you let your heart energy determine your actions in life?

Breath.

As we saw in Chapter 12, heart energy is intimately connected to breath, and the physical organs of both are located very close together in the body. The heart pumps and distributes the oxygen that the lungs take in, and the lungs exhale the products of cellular respiration that the heart brings back to them. How free can you let your breath and your heart be?

Community.

Can we see ourselves as part of a community, not only of humans, but of all beings and the planet? A powerful thing to focus on.

Connectedness.

Mystical awakening is a lived experience of the spiritual fact that we are all one, that we are a rainbow of interconnected sparks that originate in the same fire, in the same divinity.

Every day I plant seeds of love and joy in my life.

If the seed is strong, you can just plant it and leave it alone. Nature will take care of itself. However, in order to plant a forest, it pays to keep planting seeds. Trust that the seeds you plant through your heart chakra work will grow tall, even if it takes time.

Expansion.

Another powerful heart quality. If we can shed the armor covering the hearts of many of us, we can see that heart space is infinite—a cosmos of its own.

Father.

For those of us who grew up in what might be called the "modern nuclear family"—small and quite inward-looking structures—most of the deep programming will have come into the system through either the father or the mother. How much can you appreciate the good patterns, beliefs and skills you received from your father?

Forgiveness.

The heart can easily forgive because it knows that all is well. It can be a very beneficial practice to remind ourselves of this from time to time.

Freedom.

The essence of spiritual practice is liberation, freedom. Basically, we can achieve mental freedom, and emotional freedom. Liberation is when both come together. The heart is the point where these two qualities meet.

Friends.

To whom do you open your heart, and what does it feel like to do so? How can you access the kindness that you feel for your friends and extend it to yourself as well?

Gratitude.

The mere fact that we are alive means that many things are going very well for us, as we saw in Chapter 5. How grateful can you be for all of this?

Healing love and life energy fills every cell of my body.

Energy goes where our attention goes. We can help our self-healing powers grow stronger by visualizing light.

I acknowledge the Divine in myself and all beings.

You are God. That's pretty cool, right? An expression of the Divine Absolute, the Source of All, the Foundation of the Universe. Not just some little person. What would it be like if, like the mystics, you fully understood and felt that this was true? How would you act? And feel?

I acknowledge the perfection of all life and actions.

How would it feel if you didn't have to judge or criticize anything or anyone ever again, not even yourself?

I allow the infinite source of love in my heart to heal everything in me and in my world.

Healing is often a matter of permission. Are you allowing your heart to fully infuse you with its love? This may be more difficult than it sounds at first, depending on the nature of your base programming. This power phrase can support the process of becoming more and more heart-centered.

I am a living expression of universal love.

Can you believe that? If so, congratulations! What do you do with it?

I am always connected to the infinite flows of Divine Wisdom and Life Force.

It seems to be obvious, actually, but sometimes we still need a reminder.

I am complete, I have everything I need.

This power phrase helps to counteract the programming that many of us have received from society and school that says we're not "there yet," that we need to improve or achieve more until we're "good" or can be happy.

I am completely lovable.

This phrase helps to weaken the common core belief that "we have to earn love" by acting in a certain way.

I am completely present.

This phrase can be a help to us in the creation of a more meditative presence in our lives.

I am filled with gratitude.

Gratitude is a superpower. That can't be stressed enough.

I am free.

What does freedom mean to you? What kind of freedom would you like to have? What would you do with it?

I am full of self-love and inner peace.

Self-love tends to be the most difficult kind of love to achieve, as we've seen in Chapter 4. If we are able to love ourselves, inner peace follows naturally, since the origin of inner conflict—the endless squabbling between our inner critic and our ego, ceases.

I am happy, healthy and whole.

Being "whole" is a fact—truly feeling it is a continuous practice.

I am in harmony with all beings.

What does harmony mean to you? Can you be in outer conflict and still be in inner harmony with yourself? How constructive and relaxed can you be when dealing with conflict?

I am infallibly guided by my soul.

Have you ever experienced this? If so, it will help you remember that you can indeed trust yourself—and trust life.

I am open to the spiritual flow of healing.

It has been shown time and time again that the so-called *placebo effect* is a force to be reckoned with. This doesn't mean that we shouldn't use medical care when it makes sense—but holistic healing methods and meditation can enhance the effects of everything we do to support our health.

I am planting seeds of love and health in the garden of my life.

You can actually visualize this garden in meditations, and watch the seeds grow into magnificent trees, bushes and flowers.

I am truth and love.

Yoga tells us: Concepts can never be actual truth since they depend on words and individual interpretation—these are called vikalpa, unprovable assumptions. However, direct experience cannot be denied—nor can your existence as an observer. Can you appreciate this?

I bless all beings in my life with love.

Bless everyone you meet, and those blessings will come back to you thousandfold. Blessing is also a powerful technique for manifestation. If we're able to honestly wish all the things we want upon other people and look at those who already have them with love and benevolence, they will flow much more effortlessly into our lives.

I deserve only the best.

Can you believe this? Many of us are subject to the belief of lack—that if we really had the best, we would take it away from someone else. This power phrase can help you shift your perception to a reality where there is enough for everyone and all needs are balanced.

I feel comfortable in my body.

This phrase helps us to focus on the things that are happy, healthy and whole within us. By doing this, we can allow the physical comfort to spread more and more and also help to release tensions that we may be holding in some other parts of the body.

I forgive myself and everyone else unconditionally.

Unconditionality is an important heart quality, as we've seen, and it helps you breathe more freely once you connect with it.

I give thanks for my existence.

How often do you take time to be grateful for the possibility to experience this fascinating world in the miraculous vehicle that is our physical body?

I heal my heart; I heal myself and through that I heal my world.

This power phrase speaks to an important spiritual truth: the assumption that releasing and healing our own inner tensions will lessen the strength of those resonances in the collective unconscious, the universal field that connects us all, and thus directly benefit all beings by making their lives a little easier. Studies of major social and cultural shifts, such as peaceful revolutions like those in East Germany or Tunisia, have shown that the percentage of people who have to believe that something has to change in order for these things to happen could be much smaller than we might think—less than a third of the population in any case. I personally believe that this also applies to vibrational changes and the healing of old paradigms such as patriarchy or the destruction of the environment through the promotion of unnecessary consumerism.

I let my inner light shine.

This may be one of the most important resolutions—for yourself and for the beings around you. Because when you show up fully for yourself, everyone benefits. The sun does not shine only for itself.

I live in ease, connectedness, and joy.

Ease is another important heart quality. Acknowledging the possibility that many of the obstacles we see in our lives may have originated in our own negative expectations can help you find more and more effortless ways to move through life, especially if you've been subjected to core beliefs such as "Life is difficult," "You have to work hard to succeed," "It's never easy", and so on. I believe that even when things become difficult, they can remain easy in our subconscious experience if we manage to maintain our trust in life.

I love being here and having this experience.

For most of us, life is mostly good, even when there are difficulties. This statement helps us to stay aware of this.

I love myself and I love you.

One of the famous four phrases of one form of Ho'opono-pono, the Hawaiian ritual to cleanse our memories of negativity, this can be directed at anything and anyone, and used in any situation.

I love myself and my world unconditionally.

To say it once again, unconditionality is a superpower. Obviously, it's not the natural response we learned to encounter the world with. And—that's equally obvious—aspiring to love the world unconditionally does not mean that we have to give up our preferences. We cannot *not* choose, so there's no harm in moving towards the things we like and moving away from the others, if that is possible. Unconditionality in the sense we use it here means giving up the attachment to the result of our movement towards a desired outcome. Still not easy, but a little bit more doable.

I love to trust myself.

I learned this acknowledgement of the inner power and wisdom of our higher Self from Maui kahuna Lei'ohu Ryder. It seems very simple at first, but connecting love and trust in this way can open up incredible possibilities if you use this reminder regularly. Dare to be surprised.

I now allow my heart to release all negative beliefs.

Again, permission is the key. Sometimes all we need to do is tell our subconscious that it can actually let go of the problems we've been unknowingly creating for ourselves for so long, tell it that we don't want it to hold on to them. Our subconscious does not evaluate things, it merely manifests those resonances that have the strongest emotional charge. Therefore, it needs us as the "thinking self" to communicate what we really want.

I now choose to have healthy und fulfilling relationships.

This is another power statement that will not only bring you much more joy in your experiences with others, but will also radiate outward and enrich everyone's life. And, as we saw, our first task is to heal the relationship with ourselves and between all of our parts. Ask yourself: If I my inner child, or my body, or my sense of self-care could talk, what would they tell me? And, listen to them. Listening is a prerequisite in all good relationships.

I now rest completely in the love and joy of my humanity.

This one was originally created by Louise Hay, if I remember correctly. We all know that humanity has been getting a lot of bad PR lately, and for good reason. Just think of a few millennia of war, inequality, and brutal exploitation. But no matter what's gone wrong, at our core we are a truly magnificent species of animals, incredibly inventive and capable of immense love.

I radiate love in all my thoughts, feelings, words, and deeds.

You can do this one also as a visualization meditation, imagining yourself radiating light and love.

I radiate love with all my being.

A shorter version of the above phrase of power, taking the focus away from the "doing" and moving it towards the perfection of pure being.

I acknowledge the Divine in me and in all beings.

This phrase—which, if you like to use the Indian term for it, you can shorten to *namaste*— helps to anchor the view we discussed in the earlier chapters even more deeply into your life experience. If you can stay aware that you're meeting yourself, meeting God, in all your interactions with the outside world, all the time, it has the potential to change everything.

I trust myself and I trust life.

Very powerful. That is actually more of a root chakra affirmation. But I'll leave it in here since it too has the potential to bring about the quality of ease and acceptance that the heart chakra is all about.

I walk the path of love within and without.

If we can go through our lives in love, everything gets so much more beautiful...

I allow things to be simple and easy.

A friend of mine once painted this on her kitchen wall. A good reminder that things don't have to be difficult.

It is easy for me to accept love, from myself and others.

This is another powerful one. Allowing ourselves to receive can be a bumpy road, depending on how our basic programming is wired. But it is an important prerequisite for being able to give harmoniously and without exhausting ourselves. In the sixth installment of the Chakra Series, the book on Tantra, we'll talk about the forms of interpersonal energy exchange and how they can make our interactions much more enjoyable if we're clear about what we're doing. This phrase offers a possible shortcut towards more ease in relationships.

It is safe for me to express love.

This can be another bumpy one, especially if you happen to have grown up in a family where "love" was demanded.

Joy.

A friend of mine, who I can best describe as an archetypal high priestess, believes that joy works better in affirmations than love. That's because it's more tangible, more palpable in our physical sensations. Love often expresses itself as joy in one form or another.

Light.

Swedish singer FIA notes in one of her songs that people who "talk about the light while banishing the dark" are beings who walk around just half alive, "cut in half". This may well be true. But it is beautiful to meditate on the light. This does not mean that we should ignore or push away our darker, more shadowy parts. Actually, there is only light, but of course, when there are obstacles in our path, shadows appear behind them. So we can say that only the shadows show us the existence of the things we want to work on in ourselves. That's a great reason to be grateful.

Love flows in every cell of my body.

Again, this can easily be combined with visualizations or yoga nidra.

Mother.

As with our fathers, our mothers are the source of much of our base programming. Find out what you can be grateful for, what you feel resistance to in her personality, and what may have been less than optimal in your childhood. This will help you identify even more of the shadows you carry within. The beautiful thing about shadows is that they often just need to be seen and acknowledged in order to dissolve. After all, once a blind spot is seen, it's no longer blind and thus loses most of its power.

My body is a moving part of the earth, a material expression of my multidimensional true nature.

There are two interesting observations in this sentence. One is that we're an actual part of the earth, we're not on the earth, we're as much "it" as any rock formation on a mountain. We just move a little faster. The second observation is that, according to yoga philosophy, we are not our bodies—rather, our bodies are the densest, material part of very powerful energetic beings that we could call souls. So we could say that the soul is not in the body, the body is in the soul.

My contacts with others and the world are close, loving, nurturing and characterized by mutual respect.

This phrase of power brings in the concept of respect. Respect does not mean that you conform to others' narrow views of how you should be, how you should behave. But it is a helpful guide in deciding how to be a compassionate, connected human being, how to stay centered in yourself and not overstep the boundaries of others.

My heart is open to love and deeply fulfilling relationships of all kinds.

Openness is another beautiful flower in the array of heart qualities.

My love also heals painful memories stored in my body.

This one directly addresses the emotionally charged childhood memories that control our automatic response patterns and our unhealthy resonances in life.

My love cleanses my body and all my cells of negative thoughts about disease.

This affirmation I first heard, if I remember correctly, from German psychic Horst Krohne. The essential point here is the cleaning aspect.

Peace flows through me, all pressure dissolves.

Stress—at its base—is internal pressure. The more we can dissolve it, the more our heart energy can manifest.

Power.

We are powerful beings. Owning this can free us to stop feeling like victims and move into heart-based action.

Release.

As we saw, releasing tensions is important..

Siblings.

As with our parents, our relationships to siblings may reveal our shadows to us in a relatively direct way.

Soul.

What does the word "soul" or "self" mean to you? How do you connect to your core, your truest nature? Do you trust it? If you imagine your conscious self or ego being just a small part of an immense and wise energy being, a shapeshifter, how would that change your outlook on life? How would it affect your relationship to physical death? And to life?

Thank you.

Another of the four power phrases of Ho'oponopono. The value of gratitude doesn't need to be explained, I think it's quite obvious.

Unity.

Once we realize that we are all one, it becomes difficult not to love.

Warmth.

Another beautiful quality of the heart. On a physical level, our heart warms our entire body by continuously pumping blood through it, which supplies our cells with oxygen.

YES.

Yes is possibly the most powerful affirmation of all for its simplicity and clarity. What do you wish to say yes to? Can you say yes to yourself, completely?

Glossary

A

Agape – A Greek word for the love of the Divine, used by the ancient philosophers of that region.

Ajna Chakra – A Sanskrit name for the third eye chakra, literally meaning "control center". It's the seat of awareness and understanding, but also of our thinking mind.

Aloha – Hawaiian, literally, the presence of breath (Ha).

Anahata Chakra – A Sanskrit name for the heart chakra, literally the "unstruck sound". It's generally considered the seat of our soul core or higher self, among its qualities are unconditional love, joy and spaciousness.

B

Bhakti – A Sanskrit term describing loving devotion to the Divine. A familiar way to express bhakti is *kirtan*, mantra singing or chanting. The Bhagavad Gita, one of Indias most famous spiritual texts, states that bhakti is the easiest way to awakening, simpler than the other ways of yoga it explains in depth, the yogas of understanding, action, or meditation.

C

Chakra – Sanskrit, literally wheel or vortex. The Name the ancient tantrics gave to the energy centers they perceived in and around their bodies.

Citta-Vritti – the incessantly choosing currents of the mind, according to Indian sage Patanjali (author of the yoga-sutras) the only thing clouding our perception of our true nature, which is bliss, essentially.

Cognitive Reframing – The recontextualization and balancing of negative thoughts by looking at their objects from different angles.

E

Eros – Greek for romantic and sexual love.

J

Jnana Yoga – Sanskrit, the yoga of understanding and wisdom.

K

Kundalini Shakti – A tantric name for the divine "spark" within us, a sort of inner guidance or soul core. Especially Indian tantric paths like hatha yoga aim to help this energy, which is supposed to lie sleeping at the base of the spine in most of us, uncoil and rise to meet the energy of divine awareness (Shiva) descending through our crown. The result could be called embodied awakening.

M

Manipura Chakra – A Sanskrit name for the solar plexus chakra, literally meaning "city of the jewel". It's the seat of our ability to act and to motivate ourselves in a harmonious way.

Metta – A Buddhist term for lovingkindness.

Muladhara Chakra – A Sanskrit name for the root chakra. Two of its primary qualities are trust and nourishment.

P

Philautia – Greek for self-love.

Philia – Greek for the love of friends.

Pono – Hawaiian for "Rightness" or, in some interpretations, perfection.

S

Sahasrara Chakra - A Sanskrit name for the crown chakra, literally meaning "thousand-petaled". It's considered the seat of divine connection, inspiration and higher guidance.

Sat-Chit-Ananda – our true nature according to yoga philosophy: pure being, consciousness and bliss.

Shat Chakra System – Literally, six chakra system, from Manipura to Ajna. The now internationally known way to view the principal chakras as aligned on a vertical line in the middle of the body, as shown in older tantric texts. At the turn of the twentieth century, Arthur Avalon translated one of these texts, the Shat Chakra Nirupana, into English, which influenced all later international chakra work substantially.

Shiva – Lord Shiva is considered the symbol for pure awareness, his consort, Shakti, as the essence of the world of experience being perceived by that awareness. More generally, the God of Transformation.

Spanda – The blissful base vibration of the universe according to ancient tantric philosophy.

Storge – Greek for family love.

Svadisthana Chakra - A Sanskrit name for the sacral chakra, literally meaning "seat of the I". It's the seat of the "gusto for life", enjoyment, and creativity.

T

Tantrics – Practitioners of Tantra, a philosophy of totality historically found on the Indian subcontinent. The tantric movement probably originated in Kashmir, a mountainous region between present-day India, Pakistan and China.

V

Vishuddha Chakra - A Sanskrit name for the throat chakra, literally meaning "the pure one". It's the seat of authentic self-expression, becoming visible, permission, and outward manifestation.

X

Xenia – Greek for the love of hospitality.

Y

Yam – A Sanskrit *Bija* or seed syllable for activating the heart chakra. The other chakra bija mantras are Lam (root), Vam (sacral), Ram (solar), Ham (throat), Om or Ksham (third eye) and silence or Om (crown).

Further Reading

Dass, Ram—Be Here Now; *Timeless mystical wisdom.*

De Mello, Anthony—The Way to Love; *An excellent read for opening the heart energy and developing personal philosophy.*

Easwaran, Eknath—The Mantram Handbook; *About mantras.*

Fern, Jessica—Polysecure: Attachment, Trauma and Consensual Nonmonogamy; *A beautiful book about the attachment styles, not just for nonmonogamous people.*

Hawley, Jack—Bhagavad Gita, the Song of God; *Great, timeless spiritual poetry.*

Rumi, Jalal al-Din, Chopra, Deepak (Editor)—The Love Poems of Rumi; *One of the clearest prophets of heart energy ever.*

Watts, Alan—Become What You Are; *All of Watts' works are powerful reads helping us to understand and love ourselves better.*

NAMASTE

Om Shanti Shanti Shanti.
May Love and Peace
Prevail on Earth.
E Hoʻomaluhia O Ka Honua.

Acknowledgments

This is the seventh book on yoga and meditation I've had the pleasure of writing. Many thanks to all who have supported me again with inspiration, discussion, presence, and concrete help.

I would like to mention in particular:

Anette Quentin and the entire team at Insight Timer, where some of the content of this book was first published as an audio course narrated by me. Thank you for your great work in spreading and publicizing the benefits of meditation, thanks to which many millions of people today contribute daily to the field of love, mindfulness and transformation.

Thomas Young, Angaangaq, Guido Lenz, Marcel Stöckli, Aunty Mahealani, Christa Zaugg, Malu Barben, Ulrich Duprée, Andrea Bruchacova, Daniel Odier, Lei'ohu Ryder, Maydeen Iao and all the other great teachers of the heart and the chakras that I have had the pleasure to meet personally and/or energetically over the last fifteen years.

Thank you all!

www.andreasziorjen.com

The Chakra Audio Course

Touch All Areas of Your Life Deeply and
Experience Them in a New Way

The *Chakra Course* is Andreas' most in-depth online course yet and contains over six hours of audio, meditations and theory modules.

At the core of the Chakra Course are nine Yoga Nidra meditations directly out of the workshop setting, one for each chakra plus the aura and central channel. The course allows for maximum deep immersion into the self-healing powers of body and mind. Each of the exercises should ideally be practiced daily for at least 7 days to get the best possible effect and integrate the full potential.

Try it risk-free for 90 days. The course is available for download exclusively on **www.andreasziorjen.com**.

The Sankalpa Audio Course

How Can We Make Our Dreams Come True?

In the Sankalpa course you will learn in ten guided meditation chapters how to get on the track of your deepest desires and support their manifestation with powerful meditation techniques. Based on ancient Tantric principles, Andreas shows you what a Sankalpa—a heart's desire or highest intention—is and how to integrate it into your practice.

Try it risk-free for 90 days. The course is available on www.andreasziorjen.com as well as in the Insight Timer App (included in the premium subscription)

Swiss-born meditation teacher and author Andreas Ziörjen has been exploring the spiritual path for about thirty years. In his early twenties, he had a profound mystical experience that changed his life radically. As a young martial artist he traveled through Japan, trained with masters and meditated in mountain monasteries before turning to yoga, which he has been teaching in its meditative and transformational forms since 2013.

His teaching focuses on two main things: Non-judgmental mindfulness and the development of ever greater inner freedom and ease.

Andreas is the author of currently seven books and five audio courses on meditation, yoga-nidra and the energies of the chakras, all of which are highly practical and allow for direct experience of the content through small exercises. At the time of publication of this book, he is working on a spiritual fantasy/ science fiction cycle about the High Priestesses of Lemuria, as well as on an exploration of Hawaiian spirituality and its relationship to yoga philosophy.

Andreas Hau'oli Ziörjen
Photography by Luna Agneya